New Vanguard • 41

Confederate Ironclad 1861–65

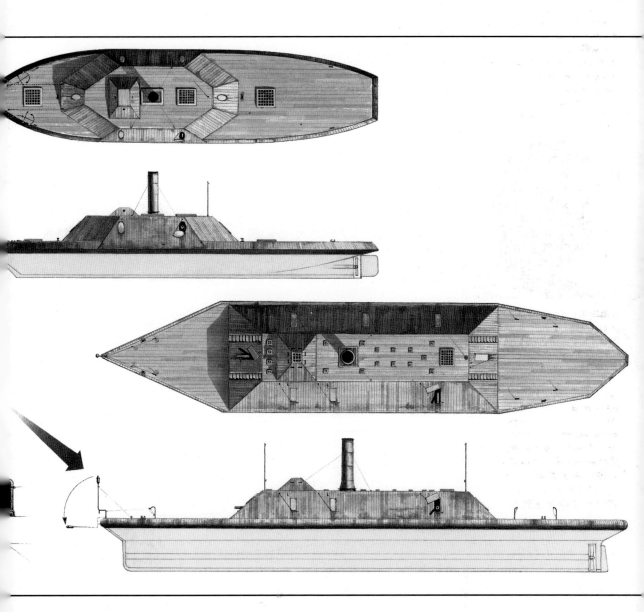

Angus Konstam · Illustrated by Tony Bryan

First published in Great Britain in 2001 by Osprey Publishing, Elms Court, Chapel Way, Botley, Oxford OX2 9LP, United Kingdom.
Email: info@ospreypublishing.com

ISBN 1 84176 307 1

Editor: Marcus Cowper
Index by Alan Rutter
Design: Melissa Orrom Swan
Origination by Colourpath, London, UK
Printed in China through World Print Ltd.

01 02 03 04 05   10 9 8 7 6 5 4 3 2 1

For a catalogue of all books published by Osprey Military and Aviation please contact:

The Marketing Manager, Osprey Direct UK,
PO Box 140, Wellingborough,
Northants, NN8 4ZA, United Kingdom.
Tel. +44 (0)1933 443863, Fax +44 (0)1933 443849.
Email: info@ospreydirect.co.uk

The Marketing Manager, Osprey Direct USA,
c/o Motorbooks International, PO Box 1,
Osceola, WI 54020-0001, USA.
Email: info@ospreydirectusa.com

www.ospreypublishing.com

Artist's note

Readers may care to note that the original paintings from which the color plates in this book were prepared are available for private sale. All reproduction copyright whatsoever is retained by the Publishers. All enquiries should be addressed to:

Tony Bryan, 4a Forest View Drive, Wimborne, Dorset, BH21 7NZ

The Publishers regret that they can enter into no correspondence upon this matter.

Key for Captions

HCA: Clyde Hensley Collection, Ashville, NC
HEC: Howard England Collection, Friends of Fort Taylor, Key West, FL
LOC: Library of Congress, Washington, DC
MM: Mariners' Museum, Newport News, VA
NCMM: Moore Collection, North Carolina Maritime Museum, Beaufort, NC
SMH: Library, State Museum of Hisrtory, Tallahassee, FL
USN: US Naval Historical Center, Washington, DC

CONFEDERATE IRONCLAD 1861–65

INTRODUCTION

The battle between the *Monitor* and the *Merrimac* (or *Merrimack*), or more properly the CSS *Virginia* is one of the best-known naval conflicts in history. While it is widely regarded as marking a turning point in naval warfare, the battle also tested the prototype of an innovative new ship type. The Confederate ironclad was a technical marvel, given the limited industrial capacity of the Southern states. Although the warship type was initially envisaged as a tool that could break the Union blockade of the Confederacy, experience in action led to a reevaluation. After 1862, Confederate ironclads formed the backbone of the coastal and river defenses of the South, protecting vital cities such as Charleston and Savannah, denying the Union access to the Confederate capital of Richmond, and blocking the rivers of the Atlantic seaboard that pierced the heart of the Carolinas.

The Confederate floating battery at Charleston Harbor, during the bombardment of Fort Sumter, April 12–13, 1861. Its production helped local shipbuilders understand the technical intricacies of the casemate design on ironclads. (SMH)

Superficially these ironclads looked similar, but their form developed through experience gained in combat. Although underpowered, difficult to maneuver, and hellish to serve in, the 22 ironclads that were eventually commissioned provided the backbone of the Confederate Navy. They were also the best possible solution to the strategic defensive problems facing the South. The creation of the Confederate ironclad fleet remains one of the most fascinating, yet under-studied, achievements of the period. This work examines the construction, design, armament, and internal layout of these revolutionary warships, and offers an insight into what it was like to serve on board them in action against the Union Navy.

CREATION OF A FLEET

When the Confederate States of America was formed in February 1861, war with the Union was considered inevitable. Following the firing on Fort Sumter in Charleston Harbor on April 12, the Confederacy was plunged into a conflict for which she was ill prepared. The strategic situation was bleak, as the Confederacy had a long, exposed coastline with inadequate coastal defenses, and numerous inlets and rivers that pierced the interior of the new nation. She also had no navy to undertake its defense. In February, 1861, President Jefferson Davis established a Navy Department, naming Senator Stephen R. Mallory of Key West as its head. The Department was divided into four sections: Ordnance and Hydrography, Orders and Details, Medicine and Surgery, and Provisions and Clothing. The Ordnance Department was responsible for warship construction until September, 1862, when Mallory made John L. Porter his Chief Naval Constructor responsible for all new projects. Mallory's vision was to counter the Union's numerical advantage by technology. While his limited staff tried to gather together a scratch force of improvised conventional warships, Mallory tackled the challenge of creating an ironclad fleet. With hindsight, his decision to develop ironclad warships as rapidly as possible was inspired, as all other forms of coastal and riverine defenses proved inadequate.

The final stages of the conversion of the wooden frigate *Merrimac* into the Confederate ironclad *Virginia*. When the US Navy abandoned the Gosport Navy Yard in Norfolk, Virginia, they failed to destroy this dry dock. (SMH)

Alongside Mallory, the author of the Confederate ironclad was his Chief Naval Constructor, John L. Porter. Working with the innovative ordnance expert John M. Brooke and naval engineer William P. Williamson, he spearheaded the design team that produced the first ironclad prototype, the CSS *Virginia*. Although less than perfect, the design provided a test bed for ironclad construction. The lessons learned would be adopted in later ironclad designs. When the war began, Mallory was bombarded by proposals from shipbuilders to build ironclads to their own specifications, and for the most part these proved a failure. By 1862, Porter and the Navy Department had created designs for a new breed of ironclad, incorporating improvements based on experience. Starting with the CSS *Richmond*, built in Virginia, Porter would maintain a tight grip over ironclad production for the duration of the war. By 1864, he was assisted by an experienced team of designers, engineers, and several assistants (Constructors) who supervised projects on a regional basis. By the end of the war, 22 ironclads had been commissioned into the Confederate Navy, and one additional ironclad had been built in France. Numerous other ironclads were never commissioned, and were either abandoned due to lack of materials or destroyed to prevent capture. Of these, the incomplete *Louisiana* was used as a floating battery in New Orleans without being commissioned, and the *Jackson* and *Columbia* were completed but never brought into service. Apart from the CSS *Stonewall*, which was built in France, all of these ironclads were built on the same principle, with an armored casemate protecting a broadside battery. The only non-casemate ironclad ever designed in the South was laid down in Columbus, Georgia, in early 1865. As planned, the vessel was to carry two 11-inch smoothbore guns in a single turret. The war ended before the Confederacy's only monitor-type vessel was even launched. Under

Mallory's supervision, the Confederate Navy performed a miracle, creating a fleet of ironclads which contested control of Southern ports and cities until the very end of the conflict.

IRONCLAD DESIGNS

The Ships

Stephen Mallory's ironclad policy began with the adaptation of the USS *Merrimac* into a casemate ironclad ram. Given the lack of manufacturing capacity in the South, any attempt to produce a design as technically complex as a monitor was beyond the capability of the Confederacy. Following a series of meetings with John L. Porter, John M. Brooke, and William P. Williamson, he decided that the conversion of the burned-out hull of the warship was the easiest way to produce his revolutionary warship. Although the steam frigate's upper works were gone, her lower hull and engines were relatively intact. His directive to start work on the ironclad was issued on June 11, 1861, and she was commissioned into service eight months later (February 17, 1862).

The basic design centered around a wooden casemate (shield) with rounded ends, resembling an upturned bathtub. The wood was approximately two feet thick and sloped at a 35° angle. Original plans called for this wooden frame to be covered by a laminate of three layers of one-inch-thick rolled iron plate, but after experiments into the power of existing naval ordnance, it was decided to use two layers of two-inch plate instead. The armor would extend from the top of the casemate (although the top ("spar") deck was unarmored), down to below the waterline. This decision to extend the armor below the point where the casemate joined the hull (known as the "knuckle") added weight to the vessel, and deliberately sacrificed maneuverability for protection. While contemporary European ironclads had near-vertical casemate sides, the 35° angle on the Confederate prototype gave the vessel an improved resistance to penetrating shot.

Her armament consisted of six Dahlgren smoothbore guns (part of the *Merrimac's* original armament), plus two new 6.4-inch Brooke rifled guns, mounted as broadside weapons on conventional carriages, and two 7-inch Brooke rifles on pivot mounts at the bow and stern. In addition, a 1,500-pound cast-iron ram was fitted to the bow, three feet below the waterline. The hull was all but submerged, offering virtually no target to the enemy. Christened the CSS *Virginia*, the ironclad suffered from a lack of speed, poor maneuverability and a deep draft (23 feet), but her

This engraving by a Confederate artist depicts the CSS *Virginia* the day before the Battle of Hampton Roads. Although slightly inaccurate, it gives an impression of the power and size of the warship. (HCA)

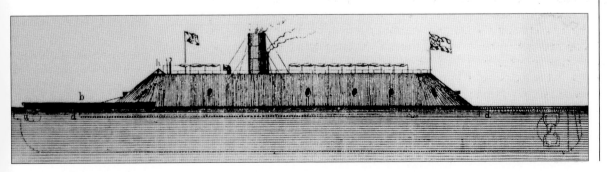

performance at the Battle of Hampton Roads (March 8–9, 1862) proved the basic worthiness of the design. Almost all subsequent Confederate ironclads would follow her basic configuration, although efforts were also made to rectify the numerous inadequacies of her construction.

The CSS *Virginia* was one of six Confederate ironclads that were converted from existing vessels. The CSS *Manassas* (originally built as a privateer), *Baltic* and *Eastport* were all converted during 1861/62, and all of these vessels had significant design flaws. The *Manassas* was converted from a Mississippi tugboat by adding an unusual "turtleback" casemate over her deck. The *Baltic* was originally a cotton transport from Mobile, and the *Eastport* a Tennessee River steamer. In 1862, the Confederate ironclads CSS *Atlanta* and CSS *Mobile* were also converted from existing vessels, the *Atlanta* from the British blockade runner *Fingal*, and the *Mobile* from an existing wooden gunboat.

In late 1862, work began on five new ironclads, designed from the keel up as armored warships. Of these, four were designed to operate in coastal waters (i.e. offshore), capable of engaging the Union blockading squadrons. The exception was the CSS *Georgia*, which was built to augment the river defenses near Savannah, Georgia. Designed by a Savannah industrialist, she proved a complete failure, and was used as a floating battery for the duration of the war.

The other four vessels (*Louisiana*, *Mississippi*, *Tennessee I*, and *Arkansas*) were all built to assist in the defense of the Mississippi River, particularly its egress into the Gulf of Mexico. Although their designs differed, they were all large and well-armed vessels. The *Louisiana* was built in New Orleans under the direction of a shipbuilder who specialized in constructing Mississippi paddle steamers. This influence was reflected in its unorthodox design, incorporating the twin paddle-wheels and box-like hull of a paddleboat with screw propulsion. Her engines were insufficiently powerful to maneuver the vessel in the waters of the lower Mississippi, and she was still being fitted out when the Union Navy entered the Mississippi Delta in April, 1862. During the Battle of New Orleans (April 24, 1862) she was used as a floating battery, and was destroyed by her own crew following the fall of the city. The *Mississippi* was designed by the entrepreneurial Tift brothers (Old Key West acquaintances of Stephen Mallory), neither of whom had shipbuilding experience. It was a massive vessel, but it was only partially finished when Union forces entered New Orleans, and the vessel was destroyed on the stocks to prevent capture. The *Arkansas* and *Tennessee I* were sister ships, designed by John L. Porter and built in Memphis, Tennessee, at the John

T. Shirley Yard. They were only 165 feet long, designed for use in the upper Mississippi and its tributaries as well as in coastal waters. The *Tennessee* was destroyed to prevent its capture by advancing Union forces, but the *Arkansas* escaped up the Yazoo River and was completed at Yazoo City, Mississippi. Unlike other ironclads, its casemate sides were near-vertical rather than sloped, although the bow and stern sections followed the standard 35° incline of other Confederate ironclads. The CSS *Arkansas* subsequently fought a series of running battles with the Union fleet on the Yazoo and the Mississippi near Vicksburg before its final destruction near Baton Rouge in August, 1862.

By the start of 1863, of the ten Confederate ironclads mentioned above, only the CSS *Atlanta* at Savannah and the CSS *Baltic* at Mobile remained. The latter was considered a "white elephant" and was subsequently decommissioned, its armor used to protect the CSS *Nashville.*

By early 1862, it had became clear that any attempt to break the Union blockade was overoptimistic, and Confederate strategy became centered on the defense of her remaining harbors, rivers, and inlets. Consequently, the new breed of Confederate ironclads reflected this "scaling down" of their role. Two basic designs, based on plans drawn up by Porter, were adopted by the Navy Department. The first of these became known as the "Richmond Class," after the first ironclad of the group, laid down in Norfolk, Virginia, in early 1862. The class comprised the CSS *Richmond, Chicora, Palmetto State, North Carolina, Raleigh, Savannah,* and several others that were never completed, and apart from the *Raleigh,* all were laid down during the first months of 1862. Their length varied from 150 to 174 feet, with a draft of 12–14 feet, and they were powered by a single screw. The most vulnerable part of the *Virginia* was the "knuckle," where the casemate met the hull at the waterline. In the "Richmond class" (and most subsequent ironclads), the knuckle was protected by a two-inch plate of spaced armor, which extended five feet beyond the inner hull all round, and six inches below the waterline.

Later variations of the standard "Richmond class" design were longer, designed to carry a more powerful armament and better armor. These 180-foot vessels (sometimes known as "modified Richmond class") included the CSS *Charleston, Virginia II,* and several others that were never completed. The capture of the CSS *Atlanta* in June, 1863, prompted this alteration of the Richmond design to encompass the lessons learned from the engagement, where Union 15-inch smoothbore guns penetrated the four-inch armor of the Confederate ironclad. The *Virginia II* carried three and in places four layers of two-inch armor, making her one of the best-protected of all the Confederate ironclads. These "Charleston class" ironclads were designed by naval constructor William A. Graves.

Another variation of the "Richmond class" was produced towards the end

The CSS *Manassas* at the Battle of New Orleans, April 23, 1862. The side paddlewheel warship USS *Mississippi* is depicted bearing down on the Confederate ironclad in an attempt to ram her. (HCA)

of the war, with a smaller casemate and a shallower draft. The *Milledgeville* (built at Savannah, Georgia) and the *Wilmington* (of Wilmington, North Carolina) were still not completed when the war ended. The latter was a particularly strange "Richmond class" adaptation, having two small casemates rather than one, each designed to house a single pivot-mounted gun.

A later development of the "Richmond class" designed by Porter incorporated elements of the Graves' "Charleston class", and served as a series of prototypes for the "diamond-hull" ironclads that followed. Although called the "Tennessee class," these vessels were each unique in almost every feature. The *Tennessee II, Columbia,* and *Texas* were all approximately 189 feet long, with a draft of 14–16 feet. While the latter two were never commissioned, the CSS *Tennessee* proved her worth in the Battle of Mobile Bay (August 5, 1864) before surrendering to a superior number of Union warships.

A second group of ironclads was designed for use exclusively on rivers rather than in deeper waters. They were therefore flat-bottomed, with an average draft of eight feet. Their design was also simplified, so that plans could be followed by inland builders who lacked the experience of the shipwrights of the Southern coastal cities. Experience had also led to a dramatic reduction in the size of the casemate, a trend which resulted from the critical observation of earlier designs being tested in battle. The trend towards a smaller casemate had already begun with the *Virginia II* where, in order to maintain a workable ratio between displacement and power, thicker armor had been added at the expense of casemate size and consequently of size of armament. Late-war ironclads were therefore better protected, but carried fewer guns in a smaller casemate. Although the size, appearance, and configuration of these vessels varied, they have all been grouped under the category of "diamond-hull" ironclads. The name was a reflection of the shape of the casemate, seen from above, which often resembled an octagonal diamond in form.

The first vessels of this type were the sister ships CSS *Tuscaloosa* and *Huntsville*, built on the Alabama River in Selma, Alabama, during 1862/63. Three similar vessels were also laid down on the Tombigbee River at Oven Bluff, Alabama, and two more at Selma, but they were never completed. Each of the two completed Selma ironclads carried four guns. Neither of the two ironclads saw active service. A second "diamond-hull" duo were the two "Albermarle class" ironclads, CSS *Albermarle* and CSS *Neuse*, both built in North Carolina and designed by

The unfinished ironclad *Louisiana* was towed into place and used as a floating battery during the Battle of New Orleans (April 23, 1862). This engraving is one of the few accurate representations of this super-ironclad. (MM)

Porter. A third vessel of this class was destroyed at Tarboro, North Carolina, before its completion. Although builder's drafts exist, we know the two vessels differed from Porter's plan and from each other in size and configuration. The CSS *Neuse* ran aground on the Neuse River in early 1864 on its maiden voyage and was scuttled. The *Albermarle* had a brief and distinguished career, engaging Union vessels in Albermarle Sound near Plymouth, North Carolina, before she was destroyed by an enemy torpedo attack on October 27, 1864. An improved and lengthened version of the "Albermarle class" was the CSS *Fredericksburg*, built in Richmond and commissioned in March, 1863. It served on the James River until the fall of the Confederate capital in April, 1865. While the original "Albermarle class" specified a 139-foot-long vessel, the *Fredericksburg* was 170 feet in length. The *Jackson* was still being fitted out on the Chattahoochee River at Columbus, Georgia, when the war ended. A "diamond-hull" ironclad, she had twin screws, a six-gun casemate and was 225 feet long. Her construction was also plagued by problems and, although launched in late 1863, she never left the shipyard.

During the mid-war years, two other extremely unusual ironclads were produced, defying the logic employed in the design of other Confederate armored vessels. The CSS *Missouri* was designed by Porter to utilize existing paddlewheel engines available, and consequently the ironclad was powered by a stern-mounted wheel protected by the casemate. She was 190 feet long, but drew a draft of over eight feet. Built at Shreveport, Louisiana, on the Red River she spent the war protecting the river between Alexandria and Shreveport. Apart from the adaptation of the standard "Richmond class" casemate to accommodate the paddlewheel, her armor was similar to that of other Confederate ironclads. Two similar vessels were planned at Shreveport but were never laid down. The CSS *Nashville* was a side-wheel ironclad, designed by Porter to take advantage of available riverboat engines. She was 250 feet long, with a draft of 13 feet, making her larger than most contemporary ironclads. She was built at Montgomery, Alabama, during late 1862 and 1863, and completed at Mobile. Described by one observer as "a tremendous monster," her faults outweighed her strengths. Inadequate protection around her sidewheels and her lack of motive power meant that she was less formidable than her fellow Mobile ironclad the CSS *Tennessee*. Delays in the supply of armor meant that she was still being completed in August, 1864, and was unable to join the *Tennessee* in the defense of Mobile Bay. Although she saw action around Mobile, she proved to be another expensive failure. As with the *Missouri*, other similar vessels were planned but never built.

The gundeck of the *Virginia*, during the Battle of Hampton Roads, as depicted by a French artist. It provides a reasonably accurate portrayal of conditions inside the casemate. (MM)

In conclusion, the design of Confederate ironclads improved as the war progressed, although a few vessels bucked the trend. The basic design conceived by Mallory, Brooke, and Porter remained the best available form of ironclad, given the limitations of the Confederacy in terms of skills, materials and facilities.

Material

Stephen Mallory's ironclad building program was ambitious, even for an industrial power. For the Confederacy, which lacked sufficient engineering plants, skilled workers, and raw materials, it was incredible. That any ironclads at all were produced was a logistical miracle, and shows the ingenuity and skill at improvisation with which Mallory and his subordinates approached the problems facing them. Apart from ordnance, the main items required for the construction of the Confederate ironclads were wood, rolled iron sheet for armor plating, and propulsion systems. Wood was in plentiful supply, although the ramshackle rail infrastructure often made the transport of shipbuilding lumber more of a problem than it should have been. The remaining two materials were harder to produce in the quality and quantity required by the navy.

Armor

When Stephen Mallory made the decision to convert the burned-out hull of the USS *Merrimac* into a Confederate ironclad, he had to rely on the limited foundry facilities available, the closest being the Tredegar Iron Works in Richmond, Virginia. The initial contract specified that the foundry roll one-inch-thick iron plates, but tests conducted by Lieutenant (later Commander) John M. Brooke at nearby Jamestown proved that a series of one-inch layers would be inadequate protection for the ironclad. The CSS *Virginia* was finally protected with two layers of two-inch iron plate. The Tredegar Iron Works had to halt production to alter their machinery for the new thickness, which was the maximum sheet thickness their machinery would allow. Although Mallory constantly asked for three-inch plate, there is no evidence that any was ever produced in Southern ironworks during the war. Two-inch rolled metal sheets laminated together to form a thicker iron plating became the standard armor for Confederate ironclads during the war, applied using an inner horizontal belt and an outer vertical one. Following the CSS *Atlanta* debacle, where her armor was penetrated by the latest Union guns, three layers of two-inch plate were used on all subsequent ironclads. Small foundries from Virginia to Alabama provided various steel plates for ironclads throughout the war.

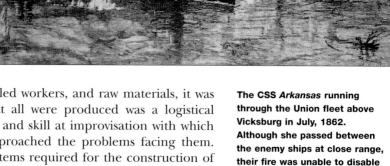

The CSS *Arkansas* running through the Union fleet above Vicksburg in July, 1862. Although she passed between the enemy ships at close range, their fire was unable to disable or even damage the Confederate ironclad. (HCA)

In more remote areas, or if rolled iron plate was unavailable, other solutions had to be found. The armor used for the CSS *Arkansas* was railroad "T-rail" iron, drilled and fitted into place over the wooden casemate frame. Railroad iron was also used to protect the CSS *Louisiana, Missouri*, and *Georgia*. Although effective, it was considered inferior to rolled plate armor.

Supplying armor for Confederate ironclads on the eastern seaboard was relatively straightforward, although delays were caused due to lack of raw materials and skilled machinists, strikes, and above all, by a lack of reliable rail transportation. As the war progressed, iron became increasingly scarce, and several half-completed ironclads were abandoned due to a lack of armor plating. Upper decks were never armored, and the top of the casemate (known as the "hurricane deck," "shield deck," or "spar deck") was fitted with metal or even wooden gratings to provide ventilation. Designers did not consider plunging fire a threat. The pilot house (bridge) was always armored in a manner similar to the casemate below it.

Propulsion

The weakest link in the Confederacy's ironclad shipbuilding program was its inability to provide suitable propulsion systems for their vessels. The limited shipyards and industrial facilities were largely incapable of producing the quantity of reliable steam engines and propulsion machinery that the navy required. Even if propulsion systems could be found for the ironclads, the engines were often underpowered and unreliable. Early in the war, a lack of suitable marine engineering plants led to the need to cannibalize steam engines, boilers and propulsion from existing vessels, or from those that had been destroyed or abandoned. The first five ironclads produced by the Confederacy were forced to utilize marine propulsion systems taken from existing vessels, and on the whole these proved unsatisfactory. Most of the handful of heavy engineering works that the South possessed were adapted to produce weapons and munitions for the Confederate Army. Of the few works that specialized in marine engineering, almost all proved incapable of building the powerful engines required.

The impetus for change came from Mallory's plan to build a series of ironclads that could be used to defend the Mississippi River. In late 1861, the Navy Department ordered the production of purpose-built engines and propulsion system from engineering works scattered throughout the South. These contractors supplied the systems installed in the ironclads *Louisiana, Mississippi*, and *Arkansas*, although some components were still taken from

The building of the Confederate ironclad *Arkansas* was achieved in primitive conditions on the Yazoo River in Mississippi. Here, the cranes of a riverboat are being used to install the ironclad's armament. (HCA)

existing vessels. By mid-1862, the Navy Department established its own engineering works, leasing the Columbus Iron Works in Georgia and Richmond's Schockoe Foundry. While Columbus produced the complete propulsion systems used in the ironclads *Tennessee, Columbia, Milledgeville,* and *Jackson,* the Richmond plant (renamed the Confederate Naval Works) provided similar components for the *Fredericksburg, Virginia II, Raleigh, Albermarle,* and *Neuse.* The navy's Engineer-in-Chief, William P. Williamson, designed all the purpose-built machinery and propulsion systems produced in these plants. Other ironclads still relied on engines and propulsion parts salvaged from other vessels, but Williamson and his Engineering Department oversaw their installation. By the end of the war, engines supplied for use in Confederate ironclads were efficient, although they still lacked power.

Marine propulsion was going through something of a transition at the start of the Civil War. On Southern rivers, riverboats were usually propelled by high-pressure steam engines, which powered paddlewheels. Elsewhere, more conventional low-pressure single-cylinder engines were used to power screw propellers. Ironclad engines were usually reciprocating, single-expansion machines, the exact nature of which varied due to the location of the cylinders. The boilers were usually horizontal fire-tube boilers with a return (double) flue. Some vessels, such as the CSS *Tennessee,* also had a fan to ensure a constant draft in the firebox. This helped maintain steam pressure. The CSS *Albermarle* had two parallel-mounted boilers, which was a common configuration, but more were sometimes fitted. The massive CSS *Mississippi* was exceptional, being designed to carry 16 boilers.

Throughout most of the war, the engines in Confederate ironclads were inadequate for the tasks they had to perform, and were also prone to mechanical failure. A lack of trained machinists and engineers exacerbated this problem, as did the lack of spare parts, and a reliable transport system to move parts and labor where it was required. The lack of speed of almost all Confederate ironclads was largely the result of inadequate propulsion systems, which lacked the power to propel the heavy vessels. This lack of speed also made them notoriously difficult to maneuver.

The CSS *Atlanta* engaging the USS *Weekawken,* while the monitor's sister ship the USS *Nahant* is shown in the distance. The armor of the *Atlanta* proved no match for the massive 15-inch guns of the Union monitor. (MM)

THE EUROPEAN OPTION

While efforts to produce ironclads within the South proved remarkably successful given the lack of industrial resources and capacity, the Confederacy was singularly unsuccessful in buying suitable ironclads overseas. Using funds raised by the "Cotton Loan" (a scheme arranged between the Confederate Treasury and the German banking house of Erlangers) and other sources, Confederate agents tried to buy or build suitable vessels. Although money was no problem, government policy was. Both the French and British governments had proclaimed their neutral status in the conflict, and the British also had a statute called the Foreign Enlistment Act, whereby it was illegal to supply or equip vessels for a foreign power currently at war without a special dispensation from the government. The Confederates had to employ every legal ploy and deception to try to circumvent the law, while Union diplomats lobbied to have it enforced.

Soon after the outbreak of the war, the Navy Department sent Lieutenant James H. North to Europe, where he failed to buy the ironclad battery ship *Gloire* from the French government. In May, 1862, he signed a contract with the Clydeside shipbuilding firm J & G Thomson to produce a large seagoing ironclad ram. As she was to be built in Glasgow, she was nicknamed the "Glasgow," or the "Scottish Sea Monster," although her official shipyard designation was simply ship "No. 61." Designed to carry a broadside armament of 20 guns, she was completely unsuited to the needs of the Confederacy. The inexperienced Lt. North was probably influenced by the vessels being produced for the British and French navies, rather than considering the special needs of the South. She was clearly a warship, and quickly came under the scrutiny of US spies and British officials, forcing Lt. North to cancel the contract in December, 1863, before the vessel was completed. If work had continued, she would have been confiscated by the British authorities under the terms of the Foreign Enlistment Act.

The Confederate agent James D. Bulloch was far more successful. In June, 1862, he signed a contract with the British shipbuilders Laird's, of Birkenhead, for the production of two armored rams. The "Laird Rams" differed from other European ironclads in that they each had two revolving turrets rather than a casemate battery. Each turret would carry two 9-inch Armstrong rifled guns (RMLs, or rifled muzzleloaders). A large iron ram was to be fitted to their bows, and the latest steam plants available provided power for their engines,

The surrender of the CSS *Tennessee* in Mobile Bay in August, 1864. Surrounded by enemy warships, the Confederate Admiral Buchanan surrendered more because of his hopeless position than due to damage to his ironclad. (MM)

although both also carried a suite of masts and sails. Union diplomatic pressure on the British government intensified as work proceeded, despite a legal smokescreen thrown up by Bulloch and his British lawyers. He even arranged a fake sale of the vessels from Laird's to the Egyptian government, and the two rams were renamed *El Toussan* and *El Monassir*, but the scheme was exposed. The British government imp-

The CSS *Tennessee* engaging the wooden steam sloop USS *Monongahela*, during the Battle of Mobile Bay, 1864. The Union ironclad USS *Chickasaw* is shown to the left of the Confederate ironclad. (MM)

ounded the two vessels in July, 1863, but Bulloch continued his legal efforts to have them restored to him. It was only after the authorities finished an exhaustive investigation into the vessels' ownership, involving British and French shipowners and the Egyptian court, that the ships were purchased for service in the Royal Navy. They eventually became HMS *Scorpion* and HMS *Wivern*.

In the summer of 1863, Bulloch travelled to France and signed another contract for two seagoing ironclad rams with the Bordeaux yard of Lucian Armand. Bulloch had been introduced to the shipyard owner through the French shipping agents who helped him obscure the origins of the "Laird Rams," and was told Armand was a Southern sympathizer. Initial negotiations between Armand and the Confederate agent Matthew F. Maury had already fallen through, as the Maury vessels were too large for the capacity of the yard. The Bulloch vessels were smaller, and better suited to the needs of the Confederacy and the competence of the shipyard, being designed exclusively for use in the confined coastal waters of the South. There is evidence that Stephen Mallory planned to use them to spearhead an attempt to recapture the Mississippi Delta. Armand had already produced similar small ironclads for the French navy. Unlike the "Laird Rams," the two vessels commissioned by Bulloch were turretless, and carried two pivoting guns in a casemate, and a 9-inch rifled gun on a pivot mount on the forecastle. The vessels were named the *Cheops* and *Sphinx* to disguise the identity of their future owners. Four wooden corvettes were also commissioned at the Bordeaux yard by the Confederate government.

In September, 1863, the US Ambassador to France was informed about the vessels, and he brought diplomatic pressure on the French to follow the British example and impound the two ironclads. By this stage, the Confederates had already lost the Battle of Gettysburg (July, 1863), and were on the defensive. Their political status in Europe was falling as a consequence of Confederate military setbacks, and the French Emperor, Napoleon III, became convinced that the Confederate cause was lost. Unwilling to back the losing side, he notified Armand that the vessels were denied permission to leave France, and could not be placed in Confederate hands. He demanded they were sold to "legitimate" customers, and consequently when it was completed, the *Sphinx* was sold

The ironclad *Albermarle* was built on a riverbank in North Carolina, a logistical feat of immense proportions. Designed by Naval Constructor Porter, the vessel was modified during construction to suit local conditions and available materials. (HCA)

to Denmark and the *Cheops* to Prussia. Bulloch was powerless to prevent the loss.

By exceptional fortune, the *Sphinx* was offered for resale by the Danish government in late 1864. Bulloch arranged an under-cover purchasing scheme involving French shipping agents, and in January, 1865, the ironclad was handed over to the Confederate Navy in a transfer in the Bay of Biscay. The vessel was renamed the CSS *Stonewall*, the only active Confederate ironclad to be commissioned in Europe rather than at home. She sailed to El Ferrol in Spain, and narrowly escaped a battle with two Union cruisers before she escaped into the Atlantic. She stopped in Lisbon (again avoiding her Union pursuers) and crossed the Atlantic to Cuba. Finding that General Robert E. Lee had already surrendered, and that the Confederacy was finished, the CSS *Stonewall* was handed over to the Spanish authorities in Cuba. It was subsequently sold to the US government.

Although the European option produced no vessels that influenced the naval campaign, different political circumstances and legal verdicts could have given the Confederacy a suite of extremely powerful ironclads.

SHIPBUILDING

Unlike the North, the Southern states had very few operational shipyards in 1861. Although over 140 shipyards have been identified, most of these were virtually nonexistent: stretches of riverbank where small riverine vessels were built by local craftsmen. The only real shipyards were concentrated in the main coastal cities: Norfolk, Wilmington, Charleston, Savannah, Mobile, and New Orleans. Shipyards for river craft were also located in towns like Baton Rouge, Selma, Columbus, and Memphis. When the war broke out, several of the local shipyard owners submitted bids to build warships, including ironclads. For example, Asa Tift of Key West, a friend of Stephen Mallory, submitted a model for an armored vessel, which could be built by relatively unskilled builders. Mallory eventually commissioned its construction, and the vessel became the ironclad *Mississippi*. The Savannah shipbuilder Henry Willink Jr. won a contract to built two ironclads in his yard, while E. C. Murray won a bid to build a large ironclad called the *Louisiana* at his Jefferson City (New Orleans) yard. The construction of the *Louisiana* and the *Mississippi* strained the resources of Louisiana, and work was constantly delayed by lack of skilled men, vital materials, or available transportation. These yards were lost when New Orleans was captured by Union forces in April, 1862.

When the Union Navy withdrew from the Gosport Navy Yard (at Norfolk, Virginia), it tried unsuccessfully to destroy the naval construction facilities there. Within months, the yard was operational again, and work had begun on the conversion of the former USS *Merrimac* into an ironclad. When Norfolk was abandoned in May, 1862, the CSS *Virginia* was destroyed, and the incomplete ironclad *Richmond* was towed up the James River to Richmond, where a new yard was set up (Rockett's Navy Yard). Much of the equipment, stores, and workforce from Gosport

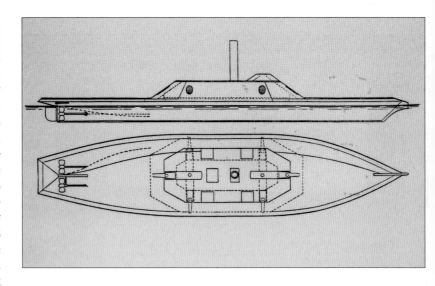

were also transferred to Richmond. During the war, the ironclads *Fredericksburg*, *Virginia II*, and *Texas* were built there, although the *Texas* was unfinished when she was burned to prevent her capture in April, 1865. The losses of Norfolk and New Orleans were a severe blow to the Confederacy, as they contained the most-developed shipyards in the South. Subsequently, the lack of shipbuilding facilities dictated the size, shape, and construction methods of Confederate ironclads.

The CSS *Albermarle* and her sister vessel the CSS *Neuse* were both armed with 6.4-inch Brooke rifles. Note the pivot arrangement for the guns, which were employed as the bow and stern weapons in most Confederate ironclads. (MM)

With an unbreakable Union blockade around the coast, ironclads could not be transported far from their place of construction. It was evident that shipyards would have to be constructed from nothing, alongside rivers or estuaries where no facilities had previously existed. In the west, the ironclads *Tennessee* and *Arkansas* were being constructed at Memphis, Tennessee, when the city fell to the Union. The *Arkansas* escaped, and a temporary shipyard was established at Yazoo City, Mississippi, so that the ironclad could be completed. Under the supervision of Lieutenant Isaac Brown, local slaves, laborers, and blacksmiths were pressed into service, working 24 hours a day in shifts. This makeshift solution worked, and by July, 1862, the newly commissioned CSS *Arkansas* was ready for action.

Shipbuilder Henry Basset agreed to build two ironclads at his yard in Selma, Alabama, and despite a lack of facilities, the *Huntsville* and *Tuscaloosa* were constructed within a year, together with the *Tennessee II*. Other small, temporary yards on the Red River in Louisiana and the Alabama and Tombigbee rivers in Alabama were also created for the production of ironclads, although they never proved as productive as the facility established at Yazoo City. Work on these western projects was supervised by Captain Ebenezer Farrand of the Navy Department. Naval Constructor John Shirley retained overall control of all western ironclad construction throughout the war.

On the Atlantic seaboard, "Richmond class" ironclads were constructed at existing yards in Richmond, Wilmington, Charleston, and Savannah, and temporary shipyard facilities were established in North Carolina to construct the *Albermarle* and the *Neuse*. Of these, Gilbert Elliot, the builder of the CSS *Albermarle*, created a shipyard at Edwards Ferry in what was once a cornfield! Attempts to create a new Naval Yard

at Columbus, Georgia, were largely unsuccessful, and apart from Richmond and the temporary yards in North Carolina, ironclad building on the Atlantic seaboard of the Confederacy was left in the hands of local shipyards at Wilmington, Charleston, and Savannah.

The CSS *Albermarle* is rammed by the USS *Sassacus* during a skirmish in Albermarle Sound. The Union vessel was unable to cause any significant damage to the ironclad. (HCA)

THE IRONCLAD'S ROLE

When Stephen Mallory lobbied for a Confederate Navy that embraced the latest technical innovations, he was attempting to offset the numerical superiority of the Union Navy. His emphasis on the development of an ironclad fleet was only part of a concerted strategy that also included the use of mines, rifled guns, submarines and commerce raiders, all revolutionary elements in naval warfare. At first, Mallory envisaged ironclads as a strategic tool capable of breaking the Union blockade of Southern ports, and of taking the war to the enemy. As the war progressed, and increasing inroads were made into the Confederacy's coastal defenses, the role of ironclads was scaled back. By the end of the war, they were little more than floating coastal batteries, trying to protect the few surviving Confederate ports from an overwhelming force of Union warships and troops.

To traditional naval officers, the ironclads designed by the Confederates were "monsters," "iron elephants," or "gunboxes," lacking the aesthetic beauty of traditional, masted warships. However, these officers also recognized their naval potential. As 22 ironclads were commissioned by the Confederacy, any description of their basic characteristics has to be general, although the development of their design has already been discussed. The majority had a uniformity of appearance, with an iron casemate whose sloping sides were pitched at a 35° angle. The basic design was not a new one; the central armored casemate set upon a low-freeboard hull was first employed in the design of floating batteries built by the French during the Crimean War (1854/56), although the Confederates improved upon this design to produce a fully operational type of warship.

The first true ironclad warship was the *Gloire*, commissioned into the French Navy in 1859. The following year, the British commissioned the even more powerful HMS *Warrior*. Both navies followed these with a succession of improved versions of these original designs. With a few exceptions, most European armored warships produced between 1859 and 1865 were broadside casemate vessels, designed for use on the open sea. By contrast, Confederate ironclads (and for that matter the Union monitors) were coastal vessels at best, lacking the seaworthiness of their European counterparts. This reflected a difference in strategic role. The navies of Britain and France existed to support the global aspirations of their governments. The role of the Union Navy was to enforce a blockade of Southern ports, and to wrest control of coastal waters and rivers away from the Confederacy. For the South, the defense of her ports, rivers, and inland waterways was of paramount importance. The role assigned each nation's ironclad warships reflected these strategic objectives.

The casemate ironclad suited the defensive strategy of the Confederacy, and reflected the realities of her shipbuilding capabilities. Although the *Virginia* had several significant flaws, it was a successful experimental prototype, and it allowed the Navy Department to develop a series of improved casemate designs throughout the war. Near the end of the war, Mallory wrote: "For river, harbor and coastal defense, the sloping shield and general plan of the armored vessels adopted by us ... are the best that could be adopted in our situation ... In ventilation, light, fighting space and quarters it is believed that the sloping shield presents greater advantages than the Monitor turret ..." In other words, the design was ideally suited to the industrial capacity and requirements of the Confederacy.

Early ironclads were designed to operate in coastal waters, reflecting an attempt to contest the Union blockade. The failure of the Confederacy to break the Union stranglehold led to a shift in policy around the summer of 1862. From that point on, ironclads were designed for local coastal defense only, marking a significant change in role. They became defensive rather than offensive vessels. This reflected a realization that the Confederate ironclad was incapable of undertaking a more demanding role, due to the constraints of its design. In 1862, work began on the ironclad CSS *Richmond*, designed as a harbor or river defense vessel. The design was better suited to this new defensive role than the *Virginia* and other early ironclads. Although designs changed, subsequent Confederate ironclads were built from the keel up for local defense.

A second reassessment of the role of the ironclad took place in mid-1863, following the capture of the CSS *Atlanta*. Later ironclads were better armored, and even limited independent forays against Union vessels were discouraged. This meant that from late 1863, the role of the Confederate ironclads was to form part of an integrated coastal defense system. The provision of mobile support to static defenses (minefields and fortifications) became the new role of the ironclad, marking an even greater surrender of strategic initiative to the Union. Given the numerical, logistical,

A hydraulic press such as this was used to press the iron sheets into the armored plate produced by Southern foundries. The standard thickness used on ironclads was 2 inches, and two or even three layers were laminated together to create the casemate armor. (Collection of Chris Henry, Southsea, Hampshire)

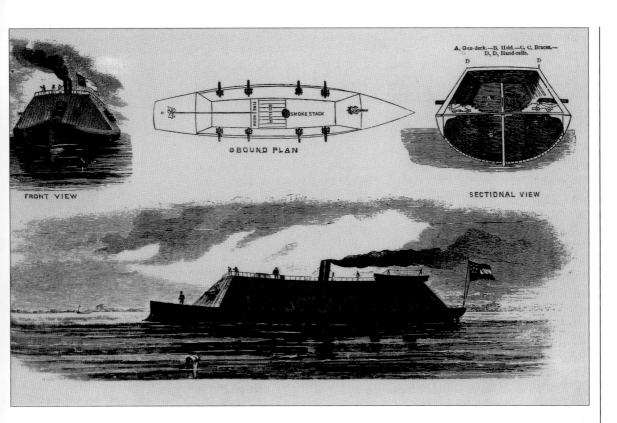

FRONT VIEW

GROUND PLAN

A, Gun-deck.—B, Hold.—C, C, Braces,—D, D, Hand-rails.

SECTIONAL VIEW

The CSS *Richmond* was the first of the "Richmond class" Confederate ironclads designed by John Porter. Their limited motive power and seagoing abilities reflected their role as harbor or river defense vessels. (MM)

and strategic disadvantages of the Confederate Navy, this represented the best possible role for the warships.

OFFICERS & MEN

The officers who served in the Confederate Navy were all former US Navy officers who resigned their commissions and "went south." Of the 1,550 naval officers in the US Navy at the start of the war, about a quarter of them resigned their commissions and sought service in the Confederacy. The decision these men faced was an unenviable one, torn between loyalty to the service, the nation, their home state or even to a particular ideology. Not all Southern officers "went south," but most resigned when their home state seceded from the Union. Those who remained were often viewed with suspicion, although the vast wartime increase in the Union Navy meant that every available officer was almost certain of promotion and financial reward. After Lincoln took office, resigning officers were deemed as "deserters," and faced arrest unless they fled south of the Mason-Dixon line. The prospects for those who allied themselves with the Confederacy were bleak, as at first the Confederate Navy only had a handful of ships at its disposal. Compared to their counterparts in the army, promotion prospects remained poor throughout the war, and commanders of major warships in the US Navy found themselves commanding converted river steamers in the South. These men had all made a huge sacrifice for the cause, and their treatment by the Confederate government never reflected the personal traumas they went through.

19

In April, 1862, the Confederate Congress established posts for four admirals, ten captains, 31 commanders, 125 lieutenants (first and second), plus a corresponding number of non-line posts, such as paymasters and surgeons. Promotion to most of the senior slots was by merit, to encourage the younger officers, a system that ran contrary to that of the old navy. Until ships were produced, many of these men found themselves commanding coastal fortifications or overseeing construction programs. The Confederacy even introduced an officer training program, to reinforce the skilled commissioned officers available to them. The training ship CSS *Patrick Henry* served as a midshipman's training ship, and operated in that capacity on the James River near Richmond from August, 1863.

The "Richmond class" ironclad CSS *Palmetto State* is depicted ramming the wooden screw sloop USS *Mercedita* in a detail of an inaccurate contemporary engraving by a British artist. (Charleston Museum, Charleston, SC)

The Confederate Navy operated through a regional command system, where a senior officer would command the naval defenses of a stretch of coastline, say from Savannah to Georgetown. He often held command of a warship in his district, usually the most powerful ironclad, although he could devolve control of these vessels to a subordinate senior officer. A lack of clarification of duties and spheres of responsibility by the Navy Department in Richmond plagued the navy throughout the war, and some regional commanders exerted almost no real authority beyond their immediate squadron. Often, the area or local station commander had responsibility for land batteries in the area.

Within the ironclads, command followed the procedures set up for the US Navy, and the captain or senior officer present commanded the vessel in action from his command post in the pilot house, which replaced the quarterdeck on a conventional warship for this purpose. His executive officer was responsible for maneuvering the vessel in action, and coordinating damage control. He was assisted by the master, responsible for seamanship and navigation, and a number of midshipmen who relayed orders from the pilot house (effectively the bridge) to the rest of the ship. In some cases vessels were controlled by the army, but naval officers still commanded them, a command problem that hindered the effective defense of areas such as Charleston, Mobile Bay, and New Orleans. Wherever they served, the officer corps of the Confederate Navy distinguished itself by an almost unblemished record of devotion to duty, courage under fire, and improvisation. Faced with overwhelming odds, they did more than was expected of them.

As for the crew, they proved more of a problem. With no navy to speak of, the Confederacy had to recruit one from scratch, and the defection of seamen to the South in no way matched the substantial movement of officers. Most of the navy's manpower came from the army, drafted by order of local military commanders partly to fulfil the requests for men made by the Navy Department. Naturally, there was a tendency to send the men who these commanders wished to be rid of, so the navy was effectively given the "dregs of the barrel," or as one commander put it: "misfits sent by lesser army officers." One problem was that the South did not have a substantial pool of seamen to draw from. Although naval recruiting stations were set up in most major Southern ports, and bounties of $50 were offered, recruitment levels were poor. Many real seamen preferred the army, which offered higher pay, or service on blockade runners, where the potential financial rewards were even greater. Ages ranged from 14 upwards, with the teenagers being classed as "boys." Surprisingly, colored recruits were sometimes employed as coal heavers, stewards, or local pilots, although their numbers and duties were restricted.

Ranks ranged from petty officer, though promotion to this rank was by meritorious service, down to seaman, ordinary seaman, landsman, coal heaver, fireman, and boy. Development from landsman to ordinary seaman and seaman was based on maritime experience and length of service. If recruits had any technical skills (such as carpentry, metalworking, or engineering), they were usually placed where their skills would do the most good. As most army recruits were landsmen, training was of the utmost importance. Receiving ships were set up at most major naval stations, and the landsmen were given a basic naval training before they were sent on active service. Ironclads were unpopular assignments because of their uncomfortable living conditions, since only the engineers, firemen, and coal heavers had to endure the stifling heat of the engine rooms on other ships. On ironclads, the whole ship was usually uncomfortably hot. Despite their lack of training and seamanlike qualities, most of these recruits performed their duties well. An ironclad in action against a superior enemy would have been a terrible assignment for anyone. It is to the credit of these Southern landsmen turned sailors that they fought to the best of their abilities.

The CSS *Atlanta* during her duel with the Union ironclad USS *Weehawken*, in June, 1863. Note the torpedo on a spar fitted to the bow of the Confederate vessel. It could be lowered into position when required. (MM)

ORDNANCE

The Confederate Navy was fairly successful in providing its ironclads with the weapons they needed. From 1863 on, except in the more remote corners of the Confederacy, ordnance was in relatively good supply. The capture of the Norfolk (Gosport) Navy Yard in April, 1861, meant that 1,198 heavy guns were available to the Confederacy, meeting almost all of the nation's initial requirements for coastal fortifications and for the navy. Most of these pieces were muzzle-loading smoothbores, including just under 1,000 32-pounders, although it also included over 50 9-inch Dahlgren pieces, among the most modern pieces of ordnance then available. Of the smoothbore guns, most were of the Columbiad pattern, a design introduced in 1811, but improved and enlarged during the intervening half century. The ordnance designer Thomas J. Rodman developed an improved version during the 1840s that became a standard form of naval weapon, capable of greater range and penetration. The ordnance developed by John A. Dahlgren between 1847 and 1855 was cast from the solid, then bored out, creating an even more powerful barrel. What the US Navy lacked when the war broke out was rifled weapons, although the conflict would serve as an impetus for designers on both sides.

The Confederate Navy Department's policy of emphasizing the use of rifled weapons meant that the navy pushed for the production of additional rifled guns. Their superior range and penetration were demonstrated by the Union when they reduced Fort Pulaski (guarding Savannah, Georgia) to rubble on April 10–11, 1862. As an interim measure, many of the 32-pounders captured at Norfolk were reinforced at the breech and rifled. By the end of 1861, the navy began to produce its own rifled guns under the supervision of Commander John M. Brooke.

The large Dahlgren and Columbiad smoothbore guns captured at Norfolk were designed so that the barrel thickened considerably towards the breech, allowing the gun to withstand the explosion of the main charge. The new guns designed by Robert Parrott in New York mirrored those produced in Britain by Armstrong and Blakely in that the barrels had parallel sides, but wrought-iron reinforcing bands were coiled around the breech end of the guns. The Parrott rifle was just being patented in late 1861, and details of the weapon were released to the US Navy before Brooke "went south." Evidently, he had access to these designs. Brooke designed his guns to copy this feature, as it made the weapons easier to produce. In his weapons, a series of iron bands were heat-shrunk around the barrel. Initially, a single two-inch-thick reinforcing band surrounded the breech end of the tube. In later and larger Brooke

The "Laird Rams" *El Tousson* (left) and *El Mounassir* (right) following their confiscation by the British government. HMS *Majestic*, shown between the two ironclads, acts as a guard ship. Built in Merseyside for the Confederacy, they were never completed. (SHM)

This depiction of the interior of the CSS *Albermarle*, during her action with the USS *Sassacus*, takes place just after the ironclad was rammed by the gunboat. It is probably the best depiction availalbe of the inside of a casemate ironclad in action. (HCA)

pieces, additional bands were added, up to the three-banded reinforcement on his 10-inch rifled guns. His guns were first mounted in the CSS *Virginia* (ex-USS *Merrimac*), and in testing the first of the two 7-inch rifles he designed for the ironclad, he fired a 100-pound projectile 4.5 miles. When the *Virginia* fought its duel with the USS *Monitor* in March, 1862, the efficiency of his design was proven, and consequently orders for more guns were placed.

Throughout the war, Brooke rifles and smoothbores were noted for their accuracy, reliability, range, and penetration. They became the standard armament for Confederate ironclads for the remainder of the war. The majority were of 6.4-inch or 7-inch calibers, and these were carried on ironclads such as the vessels of the "Richmond class." After the loss of the CSS *Atlanta* (June, 1863), larger calibers were developed, and some of the earlier guns had their reinforcing increased, so they could handle larger powder charges (thereby increasing penetration). Typically, 7-inch guns were used as bow and stern pivot-mounted weapons, while the 6.4-inch rifles were mounted on traditional carriages and used as broadside weapons.

Not all the guns carried on Confederate ironclads were rifles, as it was considered that shells fired from smoothbore guns had a greater destructive power against wooden warships. Consequently, some ironclads carried a mixture of rifled and smoothbore guns. For example, among the vessels of the James River Squadron, the ironclad CSS *Richmond* carried a matched armament of 7-inch Brooke rifles, but the CSS *Fredericksburg* and CSS *Virginia II* both carried a stern-mounted 10-inch Brooke smoothbore gun (both were rearmed with Brooke 11-inch pieces in 1864). Brooke 10-inch (double-banded) and 11-inch (triple-banded) smoothbore guns continued to be produced from 1862 until the end of the war, to satisfy the demand for a mixed armament. Most ironclads also carried one or two small 12-pounder howitzers, mounted on modified field carriages for use against boarding parties. These were almost never employed in action, as nobody tried to board the ironclads.

Vessels built or purchased overseas often carried European guns. The French-built CSS *Stonewall* was armed with Armstrong (Blakely) rifled guns (11-inch and 6.4-inch RMLs), while the "Laird Rams" were earmarked to carry 7-inch Armstrong rifled guns. The huge 300-pound, 11-inch Armstrong mounted in the bow of the CSS *Stonewall* was never fired in anger. The CSS *Huntsville* and CSS *Tuscaloosa*, built in Selma, were reputedly armed with a single 7-inch Armstrong (Blakely) rifled gun which was installed alongside domestic pieces. Presumably, the two pieces were brought into the Confederacy by a blockade runner.

In late 1862, the Confederate government secured an industrial site in Selma, Alabama, and converted it into an ordnance foundry. In May, 1863, the former executive officer of the CSS *Virginia*, Commander Catesby ap Jones, took control of the plant on behalf of the Navy Department. He saw the production of Brooke rifles and smoothbores as its primary function, and adapted the formerly joint-service facility to suit the needs of the Confederate Navy. The Naval Gun Foundry at Selma also provided guns for the army, supplying ordnance for batteries along the Mississippi River, but otherwise the guns produced at the foundry were almost exclusively used to arm the Confederate ironclads. By early 1864, the first gun was completed at the plant, a 7-inch Brooke rifle which was used on the CSS *Tennessee*. By the spring, Jones was producing 6.4- and 7-inch rifles, and 8-, 10-, and 11-inch smoothbores, fulfilling all the ordnance needs of the navy. Further guns were sent to improve coastal defenses, and the foundry even produced smaller Parrott rifles for the navy's gunboats. On April 2, 1865, Union troops entered Selma, the day before the Confederate capital at Richmond fell. The yard was destroyed, together with the Army Ordnance Foundry located nearby. During its operation, the plant supplied 102 Brooke pieces for the navy, and almost all of the later ironclads were armed using pieces produced in Selma.

To sum up, from about 1863 onwards, the Confederate Navy had all the guns it needed, and the weapons were of the highest quality. It could even be argued that Brooke guns were better than anything in the Union naval arsenal.

The CSS *Albermarle*, photographed after the Confederate ironclad was raised by Union engineers. The figure on the stern gives an impression of the vessel's size. (USN)

NAVAL GUNNERY

Each gun division consisted of a heavy gun, or a battery of two or three broadside pieces. Each was commanded by a lieutenant, with a midshipman to assist him. They provided fire control, ordering a change of target, the substitution of a different kind of ammunition, or supervised the safety of the crew. A gun captain, usually a petty officer, oversaw each gun, and his crew varied in number depending on gun size and crew availability. A large piece on a pivot mount such as a 10-inch Brooke rifle, required a crew of 27 men, an 8-inch broadside gun needed 19 men, and small pieces such as the 32-pounder in the bow of the CSS *Manassas* had a crew of 11 men.

When the ironclad went into action, the crew gritted the deck with sand, and gun tools were brought out and stationed beside each weapon. The guns were unlashed from the sides of the casemate, and powder and shot was brought up from the magazine. The officers commanding each gun division ordered the type of shot to be loaded, and then each gun crew prepared its individual piece. The master gunner stationed himself in the magazine and supervised the flow of ammunition and the safety of the gun crews. Each gun crew consisted of

a number of men who in regular ships were called on to serve as

CSS *Arkansas*

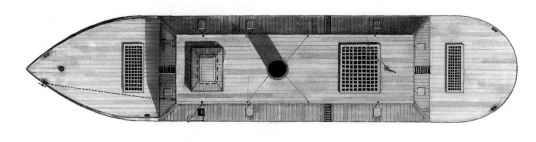

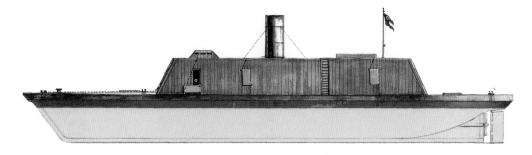

CSS *Fredericksburg*

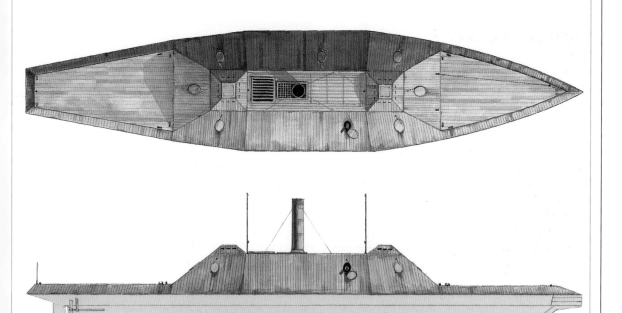

CSS Albermarle

CSS Atlanta

D

The Battle of New Orleans, 1862

c

CSS VIRGINIA
(Merrimac inset)

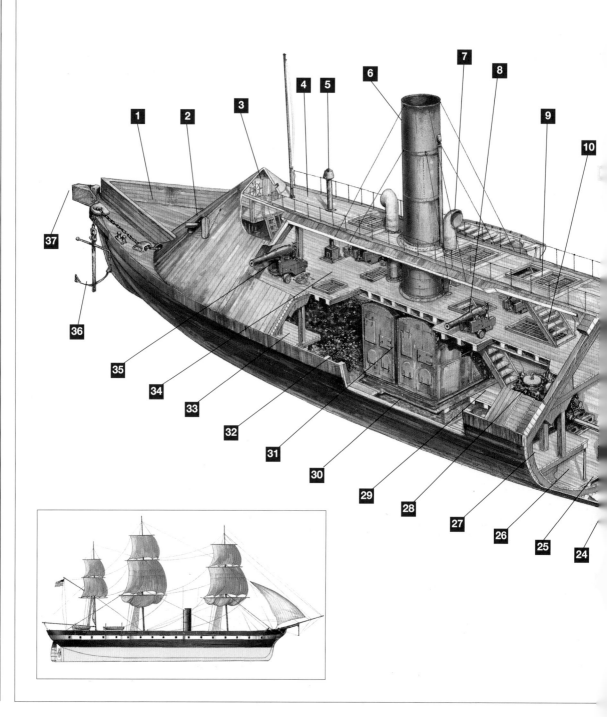

1. "False" bow
2. Gunport shutter and chain pulley
3. Pilot house
4. Spar deck
5. Stove and chimney
6. Funnel
7. Ventilator
8. 6.4-inch Brooke rifled gun on Marsilly carriage
9. Ventilation grating
10. Main companion-way
11. Powder magazine
12. Ship's galley
13. Shell magazine
14. Dry provisions store
15. Main ensign staff and Confederate ensign
16. 7-inch Brooke rifled gun on pivoting wooden casemate structure
17. Iron chain cover
18. Steering chain mechanism
19. Rudder
20. Twin-bladed Griffiths pattern propellor
21. Copper-sheathed lower hull
22. Outer layer of 6-inch wide 2-inch rolled iron plate (vertical)
23. Inner layer of 6-inch wide 2-inch rolled iron plate (horizontal)
24. Propellor shaft
25. Bilge
26. Orlop deck
27. Berth deck
28. Horizontal Back-acting engine
29. Location of temporary sick bay
30. Brick foundation to boilers
31. Twin tubular boilers
32. Coal bunker
33. Temporary cabins (partitions removed in action)
34. Gun deck
35. 9-inch Dahlgren smoothbore gun on Marsilly gun carriage
36. Main anchor
37. Bolt-on ram (1,500 lb)

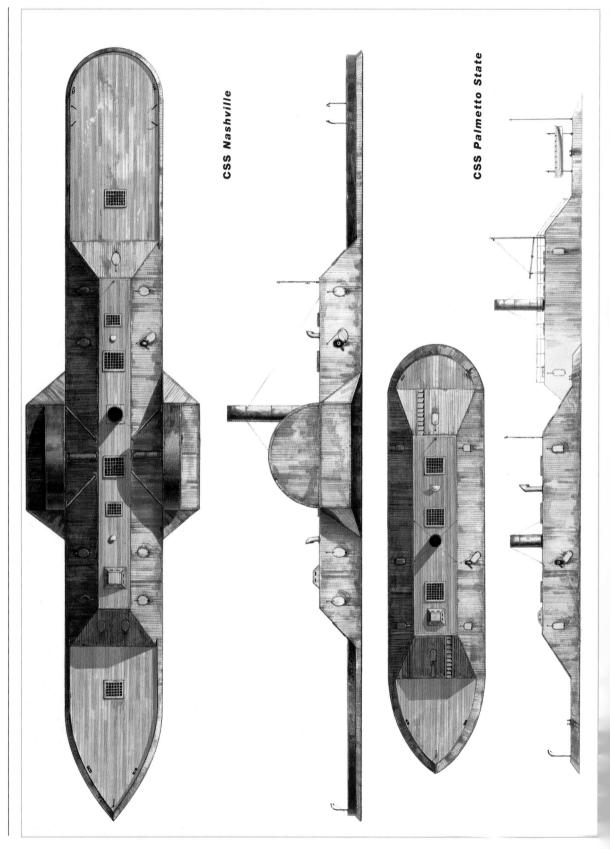

CSS Nashville

CSS Palmetto State

E

The Battle of Mobile Bay, 1864

F

CSS *Huntsville*

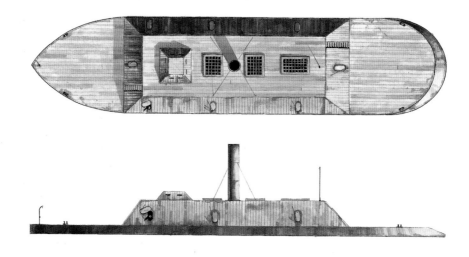

CSS *Stonewall*

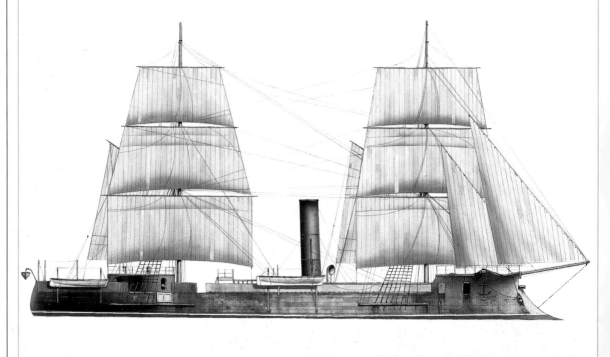

boarders. On ironclads, their main function was to assist firefighting parties or repair teams when required.

The loading and firing sequence was identical to that practiced in the US Navy. After unlashing the gun and rolling it back, the first order given by the gun captain was to "Serve vent and sponge." His assistant (the second gun captain) sealed the vent with his gloved thumb while the sponger and loader swabbed out the barrel with a dampened sponge. Following the next order of "Charge with cartridge," the powder man passed the loader a pre-measured, color-coded cartridge that was set into the barrel and gently rammed home. When it was in place, the loader yelled "Home." Next, the gun captain ordered "Charge with shot." Two shot men brought the shot or shell forward to the muzzle and inserted the projectile into the barrel mouth, followed by a cloth wad, which acted as a sealant. The rammer and loader then rammed it home against the cartridge. The gun was then almost ready to be fired. Ammunition varied from solid shot, spherical shell, grape or canister for smoothbore weapons to grooved conical shells or solid shot for rifled guns. Smoothbore guns firing spherical shot could also be double-shotted, for extra effect at close range. (A variation to the standard drill could be used when a faster rate of fire was desired, although this was achieved at the expense of safety. On the order "Quick fire," the charge and projectile could be loaded at the same time.) At the order "Run out," the gunport shutter was opened by two port tackle men, one on each side of the muzzle. Two side tackle men pulled on their heaving ropes to run the gun forward on its wheels or slide carriage until the muzzle projected from the gunport. At the next command of "Point," two handspike men shifted the carriage to left or right until it pointed at the target. On pivot carriages, these men turned cranks to train the piece. This was done under the supervision of the gun captain, who also determined the amount of elevation. He then ordered "Prime," and the second gun captain pricked the cartridge bag by ramming a wire pricker through the touch-hole, then the gun captain inserted a priming tube into the vent, and attached a lanyard to it. The gun was then ready to fire. The gun captain held up a clenched fist and yelled "Ready" to signal to the officer commanding the gun division that the weapon was ready to fire. All the gun crew stood well back from the gun, and waited for the order to fire. Following approval from the division officer, the gun captain yelled "Fire," and pulled the lanyard. The gun recoiled as far as its breeching ropes if mounted on a regular carriage, or back against its rear chocks on a sliding pivot carriage. The process

The Confederate ironclad CSS *Stonewall*, photographed after the end of the war. The French-built vessel was finally sold to the Japanese, who named her the *Adzuma*. (National Archives, Washington, DC)

would then be repeated. A well-trained crew could reload a 6.4- or 7-inch Brooke rifle in five minutes, although heavier smoothbore guns had a slower rate of fire (approximately one round every eight or ten minutes). When the engagement was over, the crew were given the order "Secure," and they cleaned the gun, secured it in its normal position and then returned the gun tools to their proper storage racks.

As for range and penetration, the maximum range of a typical Brooke rifle was around four miles, with an effective range against non-armored targets of less than two miles. Against armored opponents, the guns were fired at ranges of less than 600 yards in order to have any effect, and even then, penetration was rare at ranges beyond 100 yards. As the war progressed and gun sizes increased, penetration became easier, necessitating an increase in armored protection.

The CSS *Chicora* was a "Richmond class" ironclad that formed part of the Charleston Squadron. She differed from her sister, *Palmetto State*, by having a shorter casemate, and fewer guns. (LOC)

LIFE ON BOARD

Confederate ironclads were functioning warships, and lacked the relative comfort of other contemporary wooden vessels. They were effectively a floating gundeck, powered by steam engines. The interior layout of almost every casemate ironclad was similar. The "gun deck" was the portion of the main deck located inside the protective casemate. As on a steam- or sail-powered wooden warship, most of the crew ate and slept between the guns. Hammocks and mess tables were stowed away when not in use. Below the gun deck was the "berthing deck," which contained additional crew quarters forward as well as the galley, and berths for the officers (in the wardroom), the midshipmen's berth, the captain's cabin, the paymaster's office, and the sick bay. As the CSS *Virginia* was taken into action before she was completed, only temporary dividing partitions were installed using canvas screens, and all but the sickbay were taken down before the ironclad went into battle. Later ironclads had wooden partitions between the main stores, cabins, and office spaces. This berth deck was usually only a partial or mezzanine deck, fitted around the engine and boiler that rose from the orlop deck to the gun deck. Below this second deck, a third "orlop deck" contained storerooms forward and aft, as well as the spirit room, shell room(s), and magazine(s). The magazine was usually located forward of midships, dry provision stores nearer the bow and wardroom stores sited at the stern. All these spaces were below the waterline, so dampness was a major problem. To the stern of this deck, or sometimes on a lower deck, were fresh water tanks, the boiler room, and the engine room, with all their attendant machinery. Although exact configurations varied (often between vessels of the same class), this basic internal layout was adopted for virtually all Confederate ironclads.

Living conditions on these ironclads were virtually intolerable, particularly during the summer. Where ventilation existed, it was primitive, with temporary canvas wind-shutes installed rather than mechanical fans or blowers. Light and fresh air was provided through the gratings on the upper ("spar") deck, and through the open gunports. When the ironclad was under way, heat generated from the engine turned the whole vessel into a large furnace. Dampness from rain, spray or (even more commonly) leaks in the hull created an unhealthy, humid atmosphere. Consequently, the crew of the ironclads was prone to sickness brought on by the dank, dark, hot conditions in which they served. There was little opportunity for exercise, leading to even further medical problems. Historians have claimed that on average about 20 percent of the crew of an ironclad would be sick at any one time. In action, it was common for sailors to collapse from heat exhaustion, and "intense thirst usually prevailed."

The conditions encouraged discontent and desertion. It was therefore important to provide alternative accommodation for the crew when the ironclad was not operating overnight. On the CSS *Tennessee*, the crew slept on board a barge anchored in Mobile Bay, and the same arrangement was used for the CSS *Arkansas*. The crews of the CSS *Albermarle, Tuscaloosa,* and *Hunstville* slept in warehouses ashore, while the vessels of the Charleston Squadron were allocated barracks. This was fine when the ships were in port or at anchor, but many went on operational patrols during the night, so the crew still suffered.

On the CSS *Tennessee*, the appallingly humid condition after weeks of nearly continual rain created "that opressiveness which precedes a tornado." It was impossible to eat or sleep below decks because of the heat and humidity, and the decks were always wet . "Then men took their hardtack and coffee standing … creeping out of the ports on the after deck to get a little fresh air." In winter, ice would cover the decks, and the iron hull retained the icy cold of the air and water that surrounded it. Perhaps the worst of all the ironclads was the CSS *Atlanta*, where one officer wrote: "I would defy anyone in the world to tell me when it is day or night if he is confined below without any way of marking time … I would venture to say that if a person were blindfolded and carried below, then turned loose, he would imagine himself in a swamp. For the water is trickling in all the time, and everything is damp."

Overall, naval service was no soft alternative to life in the Confederate army. The living conditions in ironclads were the worst of any group of

The former Confederate ironclad *Atlanta*, photographed while serving as a Union warship off Savannah, Georgia. This view from off the starboard bow gives a good impression of the slope of her casemate, sloping inwards at a 35° angle. (LOC)

ships in the fleet. Battle at least brought the promise of a temporary end to the suffering. As the surgeon of the CSS *Tennessee* reported: "everyone looked forward to the impending action which, regardless of the outcome, would provide a positive feeling of relief." If men preferred to risk their lives rather than continue to endure life at anchor in port, then conditions must have been truly appalling.

TACTICS

For the Confederate officers who commanded or served in ironclads, no tactical manual existed. They were at the forefront of a naval revolution, and had to devise their own modus operandi. Much was dictated by the characteristics of the casemate ironclad. Most Confederate vessels were underpowered, and lacked maneuverability. By contrast, Union monitors had little problem bringing their guns to bear on their Confederate opponents. Apart from bow and stern guns (most of which could also train to face port or starboard), the Confederate ironclads engaged the enemy by presenting their main broadside battery to the target and firing. In consequence, they presented a larger target to enemy guns than the vessels of the monitor design. The CSS *Virginia* demonstrated the effectiveness of the ironclad against unarmored opponents on March 8, 1862, when she sank the wooden steam frigates USS *Cumberland* and *Congress* with ease. Against an armored opponent, things were very different. During the engagement between the *Virginia* and the *Monitor*, a divisional gunnery officer, Lieutenant Eggleston, ordered his men to cease firing, as "it would be a waste of precious powder and ammunition. I can do her just about as much damage by snapping my thumb at her every two minutes and a half." The CSS *Virginia's* guns were unable to penetrate the armor of the USS *Monitor*. Although the armor plates on the Confederate vessel were damaged, towards the end of the action some plates were knocked away, exposing unarmored timbers in the casemate. Although the design flaws were rectified in later ironclads, the casemate design continued to provide a target to the enemy that was almost impossible to miss. The increasing power of Confederate rifled guns as the war progressed was a response to the ineffectiveness in gunnery against ironclads, while increasingly strong armor and the reduction in size of the casemate helped counteract the inherent vulnerability of the Confederate design. Experiments with armor-piercing ammunition were unsuccessful, although the use of steel bolts as projectiles was considered but never implemented.

This rare view of the *Atlanta* in dry dock shows the shape of her lower hull, and the relatively deep draft of a typical early- or mid-war ironclad. The lack of cladding on the underside of the hull led to irreparable rotting in both the *North Carolina* and the *Baltic*. (National Archives, Washington).

A contemporary artist's view of the CSS *Arkansas*. There is still discussion about the slope of her casemate but, unlike other vessels, her sides were vertical or nearly so. She is depicted steaming down the Yazoo River after her completion. (MM)

The Confederate ironclad *Tennessee*, photographed after her capture by the Union in August, 1864. Typically, deck awnings and even huts were erected when the ironclads were at anchor for long periods. (LOC)

Early in the war, the crew organization of ironclads called for a boarding party to be ready to attack enemy vessels. During the battle with the *Monitor*, some officers from the *Virginia* suggested boarding the Union vessel, to immobilize the turret and seal the hatches. It was never undertaken and, apart from the occasional use of sharpshooters, Confederate ironclads abandoned these traditional tactics and developed their own. One innovative weapon was the ram, first introduced on the *Virginia* and used in her attack on the *Cumberland*. Rams were subsequently fitted to over half of the ironclads that were commissioned into the Confederate Navy. Ramming saved powder and shot, and against vulnerable vessels such as monitors or wooden gunboats, the tactic was a sound one. The greatest drawback was the lack of speed and maneuverability of the Confederate vessels, meaning that the blow might damage the enemy, but would probably not sink it. There was also a significant risk of damage being inflicted on the ramming vessel.

Ironically, the lack of maneuverability of Confederate rams made them vulnerable to attack by ramming, and ramming attacks were conducted on both the CSS *Tennessee* and the CSS *Albermarle* by wooden Union steam warships. A development of the ram tactic was the addition of a spar torpedo to the armament of the CSS *Atlanta*, mounted on the end of a pole which could be lowered into position on the ironclad's bow, extending ahead of it like a bowsprit. Similar fittings might have been contemplated for other vessels, but were probably never installed.

Conditions in action were almost indescribable, with the crew working its guns in the darkness of the casemate, illuminated only by light from lanterns. Although penetration of the hull by enemy shot was unlikely, in the last battle of the CSS *Atlanta*, wooden splinters from the backing caused by the impact of Union shot wounded about

50 crewmen. Damage to the engines could also fill the hull with scalding steam, as happened on Union river ironclads, and gun crews were exposed when they raised their gunport lids to fire. During the Battle of Mobile Bay in 1864, the CSS *Tennessee* was only penetrated once, when a 15-inch (440 pound) shot from the monitor USS *Manhattan* pierced the casemate armor. Like the *Atlanta* action, far worse was the effect of concussion:

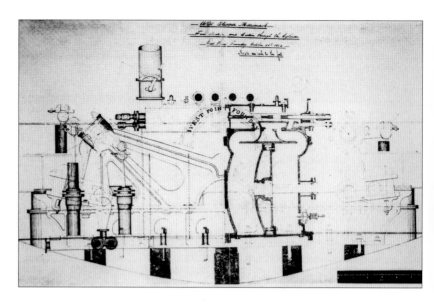

"For an hour and a half the monitors pounded us with solid shot, fired with a charge of sixty pounds of powder from their eleven-inch guns, determined to crush in the shield of the *Tennessee*, as thirty pounds of powder was the regulation amount. In the midst of this continuous pounding, the port-shutter of one of our guns was jammed by shot, so that it could neither open or shut, making it impossible to work the piece.

"The admiral then sent for some of the firemen from below, to drive the bolt outward. Four men came up, and two of them holding the bolt back, the others struck it with sledgehammers. While they were thus standing there, suddenly there was a dull-sounding impact, and at the same instant the men whose backs were against the shield (casemate) were split to pieces. I saw their limbs and chests, severed and mangled, scattered about the deck, their hearts lying near their bodies. All of the gun's crew and the admiral were covered from head to foot with blood, flesh and viscera … The fragments and members of the dead men were shovelled up, and struck below."

Although protected by a thick iron casemate, the crews of Confederate ironclads were still vulnerable. The *Atlanta* and the *Tennessee* both surrendered when the casualties and psychological pressure created by enemy fire became too intense to bear, not because their armored protection was ineffective. In 1865, the British naval officer Philip Colomb wrote *Modern Fleet Tactics*, incorporating many of the lessons learned from ironclad actions of the American Civil War. For the officers and men who manned the Confederate ironclads, these lessons were learned the hard way.

THE CONFEDERATE IRONCLADS

Although over 50 ironclads were laid down in the Confederacy, only 22 were commissioned; the rest were never completed. Of the others, only the *Louisiana* saw action before she was destroyed. Of the ironclads built in Europe, only the CSS *Stonewall* entered Confederate service.

The engines of the USS *Merrimac* were reused for the ironclad *Virginia*. Chief Engineer William P. Williamson performed miracles, but the old frigate's engines were still underpowered, given the extra weight of the *Virginia*'s iron casemate. (USN)

Stephen Mallory was Secretary of the Navy in the Confederate Government. This unassuming Floridian was widely criticized for the navy's lack of success during the war, but his vision of an ironclad fleet greatly improved the protection offered to Southern ports and harbors. (HEC)

CSS ALBERMARLE, CSS NEUSE

(Note: order of data is *Albermarle/Neuse*)

Dimensions:	152'/140' length, 34' beam, 9' draft
Displacement:	375 tons
Armor:	6" iron, with wood backing
Armament:	2 x 6.4" Brooke rifles
Engines:	twin-screw
Speed:	4 knots
Built:	Edwards Ferry, North Carolina / White Hall (now Seven Springs), North Carolina
Laid down:	April, 1863
Commissioned:	April, 1864
Crew:	50

On April 19,1864, the CSS *Albermarle* attacked a Union squadron in the Albermarle Sound off Plymouth, North Carolina, sinking the USS *Southfield*. On May 5, she was damaged in another engagement with Union warships in the river, and withdrawn up the Roanoke River for repairs. On October 28, she was sunk at her moorings by a Union torpedo boat. The CSS *Neuse* ran aground at Kinston on her voyage down the Neuse River to attack New Bern. She was repaired, but destroyed, to prevent her capture on March 9, 1865.

CSS ARKANSAS

Dimensions:	65' length, 35' beam, 11' 6" draft
Displacement:	unknown
Armor:	2" iron, with wood backing
Armament:	2 x 8" Brooke rifles,
	2 x 9" smoothbores,
	2 x 32-pdr. smoothbores
Engines:	twin-screw
Speed:	8 knots
Built:	Memphis, Tennessee
Laid down:	October, 1861
Commissioned:	May 26, 1862
Crew:	200

The *Arkansas* was completed on the Yazoo River, and on July 15, she engaged Union ironclads on the river, then ran past the Union fleet on the Mississippi to reach Vicksburg. On July 22, she fought off the Union ram, USS *Queen of the West*, at Vicksburg, and on August 6 she battled with the USS *Essex* above Baton Rouge. Badly crippled, she was destroyed by her own crew.

CSS ATLANTA

Dimensions:	165' length, 35' beam, 11' 6" draft
Displacement:	1,000 tons
Armor:	4" iron, with wood backing.
Armament:	2 x 7" Brooke rifles,
	2 x 6.4" Brooke rifles, spar torpedo
Engines:	triple-screw
Speed:	8 knots
Built:	Savannah, Georgia
Laid down:	spring, 1861
Commissioned:	September, 1862
Crew:	145

The *Atlanta* was converted from the blockade runner *Fingal*. The ironclad was based in Savannah, guarding the approaches to the city. In June, 1863, she engaged two Union monitors in Wassaw Sound, 12 miles south-east of Savannah. The monitors inflicted severe damage to her, driving the ironclad aground, and forced her surrender.

CSS BALTIC

Dimensions:	186' length, 38' beam, 6' draft
Displacement:	unknown
Armor:	4" iron, with wood backing
Armament:	4 rifled guns (caliber unknown)
Engines:	twin side paddlewheels
Speed:	6 knots
Built:	Selma, Alabama
Laid down:	summer, 1861
Commissioned:	August, 1862
Crew:	approx. 150

CSS CHARLESTON

Dimensions:	189' length, 34' beam, 14' draft
Displacement:	unknown
Armor:	4" iron, with wood backing
Armament:	2 x 9" smoothbores,
	4 x 6.4" Brooke rifles
Engines:	twin screw
Speed:	6 knots
Built:	Charleston, South Carolina
Laid down:	December, 1862
Commissioned:	July, 1864
Crew:	150

Known as the "Ladies Gunboat," as female subscriptions helped pay for her, the CSS *Charleston* served in the Charleston defense squadron until she was burned to prevent her capture when Charleston fell on February 15, 1865.

She formed part of the James River Squadron in defense of Richmond, and participated in the Battle of Trent's Reach (January 24, 1865). She was destroyed to prevent capture when Richmond fell in April, 1865.

CSS FREDERICKSBURG

Dimensions:	188' length, 40' beam, 9' draft
Displacement:	unknown
Armor:	6" iron, with wood backing
Armament:	3 x 7" Brooke rifles,
	1 x 11" Brooke smoothbore
Engines:	twin-screw
Speed :	4 knots
Built:	Richmond, Virginia
Laid down:	autumn, 1862
Commissioned:	May 12, 1863
Crew:	125

An unsuccessful vessel due to her lack of power, she served out the war as a floating battery guarding Savannah. She was destroyed when the city fell in December, 1864.

CSS GEORGIA

Dimensions:	250' length, 60' beam, 13' draft
Displacement:	unknown
Armor:	4" iron, with wood backing
Armament:	4 x 6.4" Brooke rifles,
	2 x 10" Brooke smoothbores
Engines:	single-screw
Speed:	3 knots
Built:	Savannah, Georgia
Laid down:	March, 1862
Commissioned:	July, 1863
Crew:	200

Initially built as floating batteries, these river ironclads were used to defend Mobile Bay from early 1864 onwards, but they were very slow and virtually unseaworthy. Following the Battle of Mobile Bay in August, 1864, they helped defend Mobile's forts in March, 1865. They were both scuttled off the city on April 12, 1865.

CSS HUSVILLE, CSS TUSCALOOSA

Dimensions:	(between) 150-175' length, 30' beam, 7' draft
Displacement:	unknown
Armor:	4" iron, with wood backing
Armament:	2 x 7" Brooke rifles,
	2 x 42-pdr., 2 x 32-pdr. smoothbores
Engines:	single-screw
Speed:	3 knots
Built:	Selma, Alabama
Laid down:	summer, 1862
Commissioned:	summer, 1863
Crew:	140

Converted from the river steamer *Enoch Train* into an ironclad privateer, she was commandeered by the navy and added to the fleet guarding the mouth of the Mississippi River. She participated in the Battle of New Orleans on April 24,1862, where she was deliberately ran aground and destroyed.

CSS MANASSAS

Dimensions:	143' length, 33' beam, 17' draft
Displacement:	387 tons
Armor:	1" of iron, with wood backing
Armament:	1 x 64-pdr. smoothbore
Engines:	single screw
Speed:	4 knots
Built:	Algiers (New Orleans), Louisiana
Converted:	summer, 1861
Commissioned:	September 12, 1861
Crew:	104

CSS *MISSOURI*

Dimensions:	183' length, 54' beam, 9' 6"draft
Displacement:	unknown
Armor:	2" iron, with wood backing
Armament:	1 x 11", 1 x 9" smoothbores, 1 x 32-pdr. smoothbore
Engines:	single stern paddlewheel
Speed:	4 knots
Built:	Shreveport, Louisiana
Laid down:	December, 1862
Commissioned:	September 12, 1863
Crew:	145

The CSS *Missouri* was considered worthless as a warship, and was used to ferry troops and supplies on the Red River. Unable to participate in the Red River campaign of early 1864, she remained on the upper reaches of the river until the end of the war. She never fired a shot in anger.

CSS *NASHVILLE*

Dimensions:	270' length, 62' beam, 13' draft
Displacement:	unknown
Armor:	6" iron, with wood backing (2" over paddlewheels)
Armament:	3 x 7" Brooke rifles
Engines:	twin side paddlewheels
Speed:	5 knots
Built:	Montgomery, Alabama
Laid down:	February, 1863
Commissioned:	March 18, 1864
Crew:	130

Although an impressive-looking warship, she suffered from poor armored protection over her paddlewheels, and a lack of power. The *Nashville* participated in the defense of Mobile in March, 1865, then escaped up the Tombigbee River, where she remained until the Mobile Squadron surrendered on May 8.

CSS *RICHMOND*, CSS *CHICORA*, CSS *PALMETTO STATE*, CSS *NORTH CAROLINA*, CSS *RALEIGH*, CSS *SAVANNAH*

Dimensions:	172' 6" length, 32' beam, 12' draft
Displacement:	unknown
Armor:	4" iron, with wood backing
Armament:	varied (see table)
Engines:	single screw
Speed:	6 Knots
Crew:	180

All these ironclads were built according to the design produced by John Porter, but they all differed in minor details, particularly in the placement of gunports and in armament. The *Richmond* was completed in Richmond, serving on the James River in defense of the Confederate capital, and participated in several small engagements before her destruction on April 3, 1865. *Chicora* and *Palmetto State* helped to defend Charleston, and both participated in an attack on the Union fleet in January, 1863. They were scuttled on February 18, 1865. The *Raleigh* and *North Carolina* helped protect Wilmington, but the latter vessel suffered from severe structural problems due to poor construction. The *Raleigh* was wrecked on Wilmington bar during an engagement with Union forces on May 7, while her sister ship sank at her moorings on September 27, 1864. The *Savannah* helped to defend her home port until its city capture. She was burned by her crew on December 21, 1864.

	BUILT	LAID DOWN	COMMISSIONED	ARMAMENT
CSS *Richmond*	Norfolk and Richmond, Virginia	1862	July, 1862	4 x 7" Brooke rifles
CSS *Chicora*	Charleston, South Carolina	April 25, 1862	November, 1862	2 x 9" smoothbores, 4 x 6.4" Brooke rifles
CSS *Palmetto State*	Charleston, South Carolina	January, 1862	September, 1862	10 x 7" Brooke rifles
CSS *North Carolina*	Wilmington, Georgia	1862	December, 1863	4 guns (prob. rifles, size unrecorded)
CSS *Raleigh*	Wilmington, North Carolina	early 1863	April 30, 1864	4 x 6.4" Brooke rifles
CSS *Savannah*	Savannah, North Carolina	April 1862	June 30, 1863	2 x 7" Brooke rifles, 1 x 10" smoothbores, 2 x 6.4" Brooke rifles

The largest ironclad in the Mobile Bay Squadron, she served as the flagship of Admiral Buchanan. Together with two wooden escorts, she engaged the Union fleet that entered Mobile Bay on April 5, 1864. She surrendered following a one-sided engagement against a superior number of enemy warships.

CSS *TENNESSEE II*

Dimensions:	209' length, 48' beam, 14' draft
Displacement:	1,275 tons
Armor:	6" iron, with wood backing
Armament:	2 x 7" Brooke rifles,
	4 x 6.4" Brooke rifles
Engines:	single-screw
Speed:	5 knots
Built:	Selma, Alabama
Laid down:	October, 1862
Commissioned:	February 16, 1864
Crew:	133

The CSS *Virginia* was converted from the remains of the wooden screw frigate USS *Merrimac*. Consequently, she was often referred to by this name. The first Confederate ironclad to see action, her battle against the USS *Monitor* on March 8, 1862, was considered a turning point in naval history. When Norfolk was abandoned, she had too deep a draft to steam up the James River, so she was burned to avoid capture on May 11, 1862.

CSS *VIRGINIA*

Dimensions:	263' length, 51 beam, 22' draft
Displacement:	3,200 tons
Armor:	4" iron, with wood backing
Armament:	2 x 7" Brooke rifles, 2 x 6.4"
	Brooke rifles, 6 x 9" smoothbores
Engines:	single screw
Speed:	5 knots
Built:	Norfolk, Virginia
Converted:	June, 1861
Commissioned:	March, 1862
Crew:	320

Part of the James River Squadron, she participated in the Battle of Trent's Reach in January, 1865, and was destroyed by her crew when Richmond was captured on April 3, 1865.

CSS *VIRGINIA II*

Dimensions:	201' length, 47' beam, 14' draft
Displacement:	unknown
Armor:	4" iron, with wood backing
Armament:	3 x 7" Brooke Rifles,
	1 x 10" Brooke smoothbore
Engines:	single-screw
Speed:	10 knots
Built:	Richmond, Virginia
Laid down:	spring, 1863
Commissioned:	May 18, 1864
Crew:	160

While under construction, the CSS *Stonewall* (codenamed the *Sphinx*) was seized by the French government, and sold to the Danish Navy. She was subsequently sold in secret to the Confederate government. She eluded Union cruisers and reached Havana on May 11, 1865; when her crew discovered the war was over she was surrendered to the Spanish authorities. She was the only ocean-going ironclad to serve in the Confederate Navy.

CSS *STONEWALL*

Dimensions:	186' 9" length, 32' 6" beam,
	14' 3" draft
Displacement:	1,390 tons
Armor:	4", with wood backing
Armament:	1 x 11" (100-pdr.),
	2 x 6.4" (70-pdr.) Armstrong rifles
Engines:	twin-screw
Speed:	10 knots
Built:	Bordeaux, France
Laid down:	1863
Commissioned:	January, 1864
Crew:	unknown

The Tredegar Iron Works, Richmond, on the banks of Virginia's James River. Iron plating produced at this yard was used to protect most of the Confederate ironclads built in the Confederate Atlantic states. (LOC)

BIBLIOGRAPHY

The following readily available works are recommended for those interested in further reading on the topic of Confederate ironclads:

Holcombe, Robert, *Notes on the Classification of Confederate Ironclad*s, US Army Corps of Engineers, Savannah, GA, 1980

Luraghi, Raimondo, *A History of the Confederate Navy*, Naval Institute Press, Annapolis, MD, 1996

Stern, Philip van Doren, *The Confederate Navy: A Pictorial History*, Da Capo Press, New York, NY, 1992

Still Jr., William N., *Iron Afloat: The Story of the Confederate Ironclads*, University of South Carolina Press, Columbia, SC, 1985

Still Jr., William N., (ed.) *The Confederate Navy: The Ships, Men and Organization 1861–65*, Conway Maritime Press, London, 1997

RIGHT **Naval Constructor John L. Porter was charged with designing the prototype Confederate ironclad** *Virginia*, **and he continued to develop improvements to the basic ironclad design throughout the war.** (LOC)

FAR RIGHT **John Mercer Brooke was the Confederacy's leading ordnance expert, and his rifled guns were fitted in virtually every ironclad built in the South. He was also a leading member of the team who designed the** *Virginia*. (HEC)

THE PLATES

A: CSS *Arkansas*, CSS *Fredericksburg* (profiles)
CSS *Arkansas*

The CSS *Arkansas* was laid down in Memphis, Tennessee, but when Union forces threatened, the half-finished ironclad was towed to safety up the Yazoo River. She lay at Greenwood for a month until Lieutenant Brown arrived to take charge. Local workers were pressed into service, and work continued round the clock until she was commissioned. On July 14, 1862, she steamed down river, and the following morning she fought a skirmish with the ironclad USS *Carondolet* before reaching the Mississippi. She forced her way through the Union fleet before reaching the relative safety of Vicksburg. A week later she fought off a determined attack before continuing on to Baton Rouge to help the Confederate defenders there. On August 6, she was attacked by the USS *Essex* when her engines failed. Brown ran her aground and the *Arkansas* was then destroyed by her own crew.

CSS *Fredericksburg*

Built in Richmond, the *Fredericksburg* was completed in May, 1863. Together with the ironclads CSS *Richmond* and *Virginia II* she formed part of the James River Squadron, defending Richmond from riverine attack. During General Butler's attack across the James, the squadron protected the Confederate defenses, and helped contain the Union attack. While General Grant's army invested Petersburg, the *Fredericksburg* kept Butler's army isolated, and for the rest of the year the squadron harried the cross-river supply lines between Grant's and Butler's forces. The ironclad played a minor role in the Battle of Trent's Reach (January 24, 1865), and saw no further action until the fall of Petersburg forced the destruction of the squadron off Drewry's Bluff on April 2.

B: CSS *Albermarle*, CSS *Atlanta* (profiles)
CSS *Albermarle*

During 1863, the Confederates laid down two ironclads to contest the waters of the Carolina sounds. The CSS *Neuse* was built on the river after which she was named, but took no active part in the war. Her sister vessel, the CSS *Albermarle*, was built in a cornfield on the Roanoke River above Plymouth. On April 17, 1864, the *Albermarle* broke

ABOVE **A Confederate ordinary seaman, portrayed on shore duty at Manassas Junction in 1861. The engraving was first published in *Harper's Weekly*, 1861. (SMH)**

LEFT **Gilbert Elliot, the builder of the CSS *Albermarle*, who created a shipyard in a cornfield at Edwards Ferry on North Carolina's Roanoke River. In doing so he altered the strategic naval balance in the Carolina sounds. (Private Collection)**

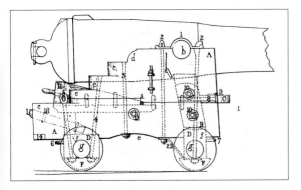

This Dahlgren carriage was a common gun mount used in the broadside armament of Confederate ironclads. The reinforced carriage was secured to the sides of the ironclad by breeching ropes. This example is shown carrying a 64-pounder smoothbore gun. (HEC)

The Marylander Franklin Buchanan (1800–1874) became an admiral in the Confederate Navy in February, 1862, and commanded the ironclads *Virginia* and *Tennessee* in action. (HC)

through Union river defenses and attacked two wooden sidewheel steamers that were chained together. The ironclad rammed and sank the USS *Southfield*, and chased the USS *Miami* into Albermarle Sound. A simultaneous attack by land forces recaptured Plymouth for the Confederacy. On May 5, the Albermarle attacked a Union gunboat flotilla in the Sound. The resulting skirmish was inconclusive, and although the USS *Sassacus* rammed her, the ironclad was hardly damaged. She withdrew to Plymouth, where she was trapped by a powerful Union blockade. On the night of October 27, she was attacked by a steam launch fitted with a spar torpedo. The ironclad was sunk at her moorings.

CSS *Atlanta*

In the spring of 1862, work began to convert the British blockade runner *Fingal* into an ironclad to defend the port of Savannah. In September, 1862, she was commissioned into service. Unlike other Confederate ironclads, she had an iron hull, a legacy from the *Fingal*. Operations against the Union blockaders were avoided as there were doubts about the *Atlanta*'s operational capabilities, but her presence deterred any direct Union attack on Savannah. At dawn on June 17, 1863, Captain Webb led the *Atlanta* out into Wassaw Sound to fight the blockaders. She met two powerful Union ironclads, the USS *Weehawkeen* and the *Nahant*, both armed with 15-inch guns. The *Atlanta* ran aground at the start of the engagement and, unable to defend herself against the enemy, she surrendered within 20 minutes.

C: CSS *Manassas*, CSS *Louisiana*
The Battle of New Orleans, 1862

In the spring of 1862, the only operational defenses of New Orleans and the Mississippi Delta were the two forts of Fort St. Philip and Fort Jackson, plus a motley collection of hastily armed riverboats. The only operational ironclad available was the CSS *Manassas*, a privately built privateer which had been commandeered by the Confederate Navy. Her unusual "cigar-shaped" hull was only lightly protected, and her armament was limited to a single 32-pounder gun and a ram. Two other ironclads, the *Mississippi* and the *Louisiana*, were still being completed in the city's shipyards.

On the night of April 23, Admiral Farragut led his fleet of 23 wooden Union warships up the Mississippi and broke through the line of obstructions that crossed the river below the forts. The *Louisiana* had been towed into position near Fort St. Philip, where she acted as an immobile floating battery. Five fire-rafts were unleashed on the Union fleet, then both sides closed for a melee fought at short range. The *Manassas* rammed two Union warships before being forced aground, her crew escaping ashore.

The plate depicts the *Manassas* heading towards Farragut's flagship the USS *Hartford*, as the Union vessel is busy fending off a fire-raft. In the background, the *Louisiana* and Fort St. Philip direct a heavy fire against the Union screw sloop. Farragut recorded that it seemed "as if all the artillery of heaven were playing on the earth." A ramming attack by the USS *Mississippi* forced the *Manassas* to veer away, then she became embroiled in her own private battle against four enemy gunboats. The *Hartford* escaped to fight another day.

D: CSS *Virginia* (ex-USS *Merrimac*)
(cutaway view)

Secretary of the Navy Stephen Mallory decided to convert the burned-out hull of the wooden steam frigate *Merrimac* (or *Merrimack*) into the first Confederate ironclad. A committee headed by John L. Porter designed this prototype, which used the lower hull and machinery of the frigate, but from the waterline up, the design was completely revolutionary. A wooden casemate was covered with two layers of two-inch-thick iron plating. Her armament consisted of six 9-inch smoothbore Dahlgrens, two 6.4-inch Brooke rifles, with 7-inch Brooke rifles at the bow and stern. Although well armed and protected, her greatest drawbacks were her propulsion and steering systems. At best, she was capable of making five knots, and her turning circle was twice that of the original Merrimac. Her steering chains also ran across the exposed deck, and were therefore extremely vulnerable.

On March 8, 1862, she sortied out of Norfolk into Hampton Roads. Impervious to Union shot, she rammed and sank the USS *Cumberland*, then set the USS *Congress* on fire, and returned to Norfolk. The following day she tried to

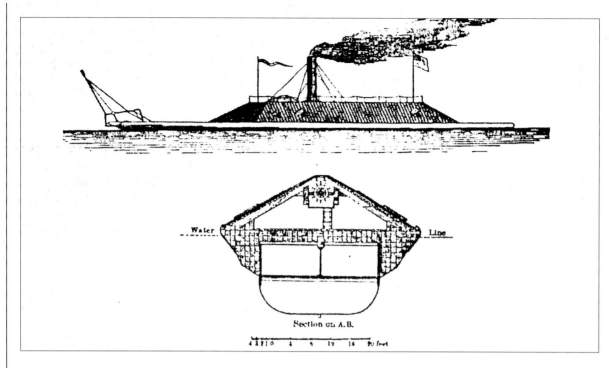

Plan and cross-section of the CSS *Atlanta*, drawn after her capture by two Union monitors at Wassaw Sound, south of Savannah on June 17, 1863. Note the spar torpedo carried on her bow. (USN)

complete her one-sided engagement, but instead she met the USS *Monitor*. The clash between the two ironclads was inconclusive, but proved to be a revolutionary moment in naval warfare. The Virginia failed to break the blockade, but every subsequent time she sortied, the Union ships fled. Any victory was fleeting, as on May 11, the Confederates abandoned Norfolk. Unable to steam up the James River to safety in Richmond, the ironclad was destroyed by her own crew. Although destroyed, her legacy lived on, and the lessons learned from her construction and performance were applied to subsequent generations of Confederate ironclads.

E: CSS *Nashville*, CSS *Palmetto State*
CSS *Nashville*
The *Nashville* was an unusual warship; together with the CSS *Baltic* and *Missouri*, she used a paddlewheel mechanism for propulsion. She was built in Montgomery, Alabama, and then taken for completion to Mobile, although the supply of materials delayed her commissioning. Armor plating was taken from the condemned *Baltic*, as armor plating was unavailable elsewhere. Although commissioned in March, 1864, she was only ready for active service in September. Her broadside armament consisted of 7-inch rifles, weapons that were usually reserved for bow and stern guns on Confederate ironclads. The light armor plating over her side paddlewheel boxes made her vulnerable, and her slow speed made her virtually useless in tidal waters. She participated in the defense of Mobile in March, 1865, then escaped up the Tombigbee River. She remained there until the end of the war.

CSS *Palmetto State*
The *Palmetto State* and her sister ship the *Chicora* were built with great speed during 1862, as the inhabitants of Charleston considered that a Union attack was imminent. By November, both ironclads were in service, and together they formed the backbone of the Charleston Squadron. Commodore Ingraham used them as part of a coordinated defense, which included Fort Sumter and other coastal defenses. Both were "Richmond class" ironclads, although they varied from the original vessel of the class. On January 31, 1863, the ironclads attacked the blockading squadron, the *Palmetto State* ramming the wooden USS *Mercedita*, forcing it to surrender, while the *Chicora* attacked the USS *Keystone State*. The ironclads continued to defend the harbor until the city fell to General Sherman. The two vessels were blown up on February 18, 1865, together with the ironclads CSS *Charleston* and the unfinished *Columbia*.

F: CSS *Tennessee*
The Battle of Mobile Bay, 1864
A Union attack on Mobile Bay had been expected throughout the war, but in August, 1864, the only Confederate ironclad capable of operating in the Bay was the CSS *Tennessee II*. She was the flagship of Admiral Buchanan, who last saw action in the CSS *Virginia*'s fight against the USS *Monitor* two years earlier, and she was assisted by two wooden paddlewheel gunboats. A string of fortifications, centered around the brick Fort Morgan and Fort Gaines, protected the entrances to the bay, while underwater obstructions and torpedoes (mines) were strung across the main ship channel.

At dawn on August 5, 1864, Admiral Farragut led his fleet past Fort Morgan, with the ships lashed together in pairs. The USS *Brooklyn* led the column, followed by the USS *Hartford*. Four monitors formed a separate column. One, the monitor USS *Tecumseh*, struck a mine and sank. After the two

A 6.4" Brooke rifle pictured outside the old Richmond National Battlefield Park Headquarters (Chimborazo site). This was the standard broadside weapon fitted in most Confederate ironclads. (author)

Confederate gunboats were driven off, the majority of the Union fleet attacked the ironclad, the *Tennessee*. She was rammed by the wooden warships, USS *Monongahela* and the *Lackawanna*, without damage, her fire crippling the Union ships. At one point, the *Hartford* and the *Tennessee* lay alongside each other, exchanging broadsides at point-blank range. The three surviving Union monitors entered the fray, their guns repeatedly slamming projectiles into the *Tennessee*'s armored casemate. Her steering gear was shot away, and her gunport shutters jammed. Helpless, the *Tennessee*'s crew surrendered to the inevitable. The plate depicts the *Tennessee* in the foreground, attacked by (from the left), the USS *Chicasaw*, *Monongahela*, *Kennebec*, and the *Hartford*. Another six Union warships were equally busy attacking the ironclad off her bow and starboard side.

G: CSS *Huntsville*, CSS *Stonewall*
CSS *Huntsville*
The CSS *Huntsville* and her sister ship the CSS *Tuscaloosa* were built in the summer of 1862 at Selma, Alabama, and were originally designed as floating batteries. Other sister ships were never completed. Although the city contained an ironworks and a gun foundry, construction was dogged by problems, and in the spring of 1863 the two vessels were still

not complete. They were taken downriver to Mobile for fitting out, and both were commissioned by mid-summer. Both were used in the defense of Mobile, as their slow speed and poor seaworthiness made them unsuitable for use in Mobile Bay. Following the Battle of Mobile Bay (August 5, 1864), the ironclads provided the only effective naval defense of the city until Mobile's fall in April, 1865. The vessels retreated up the Tombigbee River, only to be scuttled on April 12.

CSS *Stonewall*
The only Confederate ironclad commissioned outside the Confederacy, the *Stonewall* was built in Bordeaux, at the Armand shipyard. Before her completion, she was impounded by the French government, and then sold to Denmark. By luck, the Danes reneged, and Armand's agents secretly resold the vessel to the Confederacy. In January, 1865, she was transferred at sea to Confederate command, and later put into the Spanish port of El Ferrol for repairs. Trapped by two Union cruisers (the USS *Niagara* and *Sacramento*), she sailed out to fight her way past them, but they declined to fight. At Lisbon, the *Stonewall* escaped her blockaders due to the observation of neutrality laws. On May 11, she reached Havana, where her crew discovered that the war was over. She was duly surrendered to the Spanish.

A pivot carriage of this kind was frequently used to mount bow and stern guns on Confederate ironclads. The gun could be traversed through 90° to each side, and the rear portion of the carriage absorbed the recoil. Brooke rifles were commonly mounted on these carriages. (HEC)

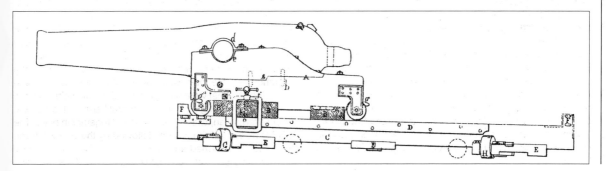

INDEX

COMPANION SERIES FROM OSPREY

ESSENTIAL HISTORIES
Spanning history from ancient times to the present day, Essential Histories represent a fascinating and unique approach to the study of human conflict. Each volume provides a complete guide to one major war or theater of war; its motives, methods and repercussions.

MEN-AT-ARMS
An unrivaled source of information on the organization, uniforms and equipment of the world's fighting men, past and present. The series covers hundreds of subjects spanning 5,000 years of history. Each 48-page book includes concise texts packed with specific information, some 40 photos, maps and diagrams, and eight color plates of uniformed figures.

ELITE
Detailed information on the uniforms and insignia of the world's most famous military forces. Each 64-page book contains some 50 photographs and diagrams, and 12 pages of full-color artwork.

WARRIOR
Definitive analysis of the armour, weapons, tactics and motivation of the fighting men of history. Each 64-page book contains cutaways and exploded artwork of the warrior's weapons and armor.

CAMPAIGN
Concise, authoritative accounts of history's decisive military encounters. Each 96-page book contains over 90 illustrations including maps, orders of battle, color plates, and three-dimensional battle maps.

ORDER OF BATTLE
The most detailed information ever published on the units which fought history's great battles. Each 96-page book contains comprehensive organization diagrams supported by ultra-detailed color maps. Each title also includes a large fold-out base map.

AIRCRAFT OF THE ACES
Focuses exclusively on the elite pilots of major air campaigns, and includes unique interviews with surviving aces sourced specifically for each volume. Each 96-page volume contains up to 40 specially commissioned artworks, unit listings, new scale plans and the best archival photography available.

COMBAT AIRCRAFT
Technical information from the world's leading aviation writers on the aircraft types flown. Each 96-page volume contains up to 40 specially commissioned artworks, unit listings, new scale plans and the best archival photography available.

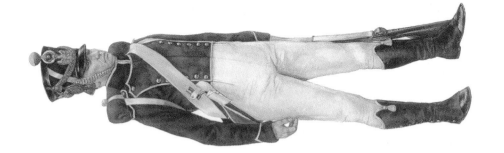

OSPREY
PUBLISHING

FIND OUT MORE ABOUT OSPREY

❑ Please send me a FREE trial issue
of Osprey Military Journal

❑ Please send me the latest listing of Osprey's publications

❑ I would like to subscribe to Osprey's e-mail newsletter

Title/rank

Name

Address

Postcode/zip   state/country

e-mail

Which book did this card come from?

❑ I am interested in military history

My preferred period of military history is _____

❑ I am interested in military aviation

My preferred period of military aviation is _____

I am interested in *(please tick all that apply)*

❑ general history   ❑ militaria   ❑ model making
❑ wargaming   ❑ re-enactment

Please send to:

USA & Canada: Osprey Direct USA, c/o Motorbooks
International, P.O. Box 1, 729 Prospect Avenue, Osceola,
WI 54020

UK, Europe and rest of world:
Osprey Direct UK, P.O. Box 140, Wellingborough, Northants,
NN8 2FA, United Kingdom

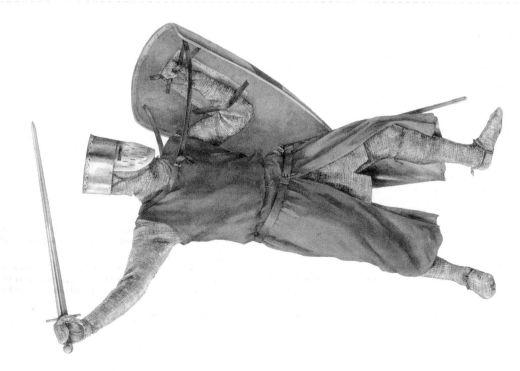

OSPREY
PUBLISHING

www.ospreypublishing.com

call our telephone hotline
for a free information pack

USA & Canada: 1-800-458-0454
UK, Europe and rest of world call:
+44 (0) 1933 443 863

Young Guardsman
Figure taken from *Warrior 22:
Imperial Guardsman 1799–1815*
Published by Osprey
Illustrated by Christa Hook

Knight, c.1190
Figure taken from *Warrior 1: Norman Knight 950 – 1204AD*
Published by Osprey
Illustrated by Christa Hook

POSTCARD